BUREAUCR.
POLITICS
AND
PUBLIC POLI(

D0721153

Bureaucracy,
Politics,
and
Public Policy
Second Edition

Francis E. Rourke
Johns Hopkins University

LITTLE, BROWN AND COMPANY · BOSTON · TORONTO

LIBRARY OF CONGRESS CATALOG CARD NO. 75-26435

THIRD PRINTING

*Published simultaneously in Canada
by Little, Brown & Company (Canada) Limited*

PRINTED IN THE UNITED STATES OF AMERICA

For Kathy, Steve,
and Anne

Preface to the Second Edition

Since the first edition of this book was published, there has been a great burst of interest in public policy and the way in which it is made. This is reflected in a variety of developments, including the increasing number of public policy courses now being taught in colleges and universities and the establishment of separate career programs in the public policy area.

But the development that made a second edition of this book seem particularly useful was a vast expansion in our knowledge of public policy. We know a good deal more about policy-making than we did seven years ago, as a result not only of recent scholarship but also of certain traumatic experiences the country endured in domestic as well as in foreign affairs in recent years. This edition seeks to incorporate some of what we have learned into the framework of analysis presented in the earlier book.

A second purpose of this edition is to bring the role and significance of bureaucratic organizations in the policy process into sharper focus. The record of policy failure in recent years has been a long one, and it has led to an intensive search for the factors that make things go wrong when societies set out to deal with their problems.

Bureaucracy has perhaps been more often identified as the culprit for policy failure in recent years than any other factor in the governmental process. This is not hard to understand. If policy goals are not achieved, who better to blame than the organizations charged with their attainment? In a world in which bureaucracy is a visible presence in virtually every sphere of activity, it is natural that it should become a universal scapegoat.

This edition attempts to identify the ways in which bureaucratic organizations do indeed contribute to policy failures. At the same time, it seeks to make clear that bureaucracies function in a larger political system in which other forces and factors contribute to failures for which executive agencies are often blamed.

As in the case of the first edition, the analysis presented here has benefitted greatly from the work of others. Academic writing is perhaps best described — in words that Robert Frost has written — as an enterprise in which "men [and women] work together, . . . whether they work together or apart."

But I would also like to mention and give special thanks to those who read and commented on these pages when they were being revised: Charles D. Cary, Dale Rogers Marshall, John McGlennon, Michael Nelson, and Paul Schulman. They did their best to make this a better book, but as students of bureaucracy so well know, successful implementation of even the best advice cannot always be counted on.

I would also like to express my appreciation to Evelyn Scheulen, who typed the manuscript for this edition, with her usual skill.

At Little, Brown, Rick Boyer provided both help and encouragement while this project was being undertaken. As copyeditor, Mary A. De Vries was of invaluable assistance.

Preface to the First Edition

One approach to public bureaucracy that has won increasing favor in recent years is to look upon government agencies as part of the family of organizations — sharing common problems with churches, factories, trade unions, and a host of other private institutions. The emergence of an organization theory with a scope as wide as society itself has had an enormously stimulating effect upon the study of public administration. It has introduced a whole new range of explanatory concepts as a guide to understanding the behavior of public officials.

At the same time, however, an appreciation of the characteristics that public agencies share with private organizations should not be allowed to obscure the unique function of these agencies as instruments of the state intimately involved in the development and execution of public policy. It is the role of bureaucracy in the policy process that is at the center of concern in this book. For it is in the crucible of administrative politics today that public policy is mainly hammered out, through bargaining, negotiation, and conflict among appointed rather than elected officials. The bureaucratization of the policy process is particularly pronounced in defense and foreign affairs, but it reaches into domestic policy as well. The design and operation of the policy systems in which bureaucracies participate has thus become a primary item on the agenda of contemporary political science.

This study is largely based on materials drawn from the American experience. Consequently, it applies more directly to the interaction between bureaucracy and public policy in the United States than it does to other political systems. Certain features of the policy process that are examined, especially the extensive involvement of executive agencies in the task of creating and nursing a constituency, are almost distinctively American. In the so-called emerging nations, for example — where political institutions are characteristically quite undeveloped — bureaucratic power tends to rest on a monopoly of expertise and command of the formal apparatus of the state. However, the American pattern has many parallels elsewhere, and, as the most advanced industrial system in the world, it may well represent a model toward which other societies will eventually evolve.

Needless to say, I have incurred a great many debts in the course of preparing this manuscript. This debt is obvious in the case of the authors cited in the footnotes and bibliography. Without their assistance, the book could not have been written.

Less obvious is the contribution of those whose assistance has been more personal. Without involving them in any way in mistakes or failures on my part, I would like to express my gratitude to Professors Alan Altshuler, Jerome Gilison, and Robert W. Tucker for reading the manuscript and making many suggestions toward its improvement.

In working on this study, I had the assistance of three very able graduate assistants, Virginia Ermer, Aubrey King, and Paul Lutzker. Mrs. Ermer helped proofread the manuscript, Mr. King did much of the work involved in preparing the bibliography that appears at the end of the book, and Mr. Lutzker's resourcefulness was a constant asset to me.

All the graduate students in my seminar in public administration read the manuscript and gave me the benefit of their sagacious and irreverent comments.

With her customary and still somewhat incredible efficiency, Mrs. Catherine Grover typed the manuscript, correcting my errors as she went along.

Finally, at Little, Brown, I would like to record my appreciation to Donald R. Hammonds, who started me on this project, and David L. Giele, who helped bring it to completion.

Contents

BUREAUCRACY,
POLITICS,
AND
PUBLIC POLICY

CHAPTER ONE

Introduction:
Bureaucrats
and Policy-Making

The belief that power in the modern state has come increasingly to be centered in the corridors of bureaucracy is more often asserted or assumed than examined. This book is an inquiry into the nature of the role that bureaucrats play in making policy decisions in contemporary government. It focuses both on the roots of bureaucratic power — the source from which administrative agencies derive their influence on the policy process — and on the distinctive problems that arise when policy-making is carried on within a setting in which executive organizations play a major role.

In the United States, at least, it is possible to assimilate the study of administrative policy-making into the traditional group analysis of political life. Agencies provide channels of "access" through which segments of the public can advance or protect their interests in the executive branch in much the same way as they pursue their goals through other governmental institutions — the political parties, the legislature, and even the judiciary.[1] From this perspective of bureaucratic politics, an agency's power depends upon its ability to command the support of fervent and substantial clientele groups, or upon its ability to maneuver successfully in the pursuit of its interests within the legislative or executive branch of government.

Certainly, there is no disputing the fact that a great deal of administrative influence can be explained within this framework of group theory. It is the agitation of outside groups that commonly leads to the establishment of executive agencies, and agencies and

1

groups are thereafter bound together on a day-to-day basis through a wide variety of mutually rewarding relationships. This is especially true in the case of executive agencies administering domestic programs that serve special clientele groups, where it is often true to say that administrative influence rests entirely on public support, or, as one author puts it, "power is organized around constituency." [2]

However, this is not a complete picture of the bureaucratic role in the policy process. It is not adequate as a description of bureaucratic power in American administration, even though government agencies in this country have very wide-ranging involvement in the political process, and it is certainly not suitable as a description of bureaucracy in Western European government, where, by law and tradition, executive agencies are considerably more insulated from the play of ordinary political forces. Political activity such as the negotiation of alliances with outside groups can be a useful source of power for any administrative agency, but it is by no means the only source of administrative influence.

The fact of the matter is that bureaucracy is more than a mere conduit through which the values and aspirations of various segments of the community are incorporated into public policy. Within its own ranks, public bureaucracy numbers a wide variety of highly organized and technically trained professional personnel, whose knowledge and skills powerfully influence the shape of official decision. While bureaucratic policy-making in many fields has been primarily a reflection of a system of external group pressures, there are other areas such as science and national defense where the expertise and interests of bureaucratic organizations have themselves been controlling factors in the evolution of public policy. In most cases policy decisions within bureaucracy represent the outcome of a process of interaction between these two sources of power — the needs or aspirations of groups within the community with which executive agencies are allied, as well as the expertise and interests of bureaucrats themselves.

In terms of its impact on its environment, the rise of bureaucracy in the American political system has both aggravated and altered inequalities of power within the private sector of society. In some cases, executive agencies have simply echoed the views of major economic interests, in this way augmenting the advantages of those already powerful. In other instances, however, public organizations have been vigorous protagonists of groups at the lower end of the scale in terms of wealth or power. One of the historic functions of bureaucracy in American society has been to provide a means of effective expression in policy deliberations for community groups that are inarticulate, poorly organized, or for some other reason unable to speak for themselves. With administrative help, these stepchildren of the political system may acquire a political equality with other groups that they could never hope to attain through the ordinary processes of politics alone. Bureaucrats may thus alter as well as mirror the patterns of group strength that play so important a role in the development of public policy.

In addition to these cases where public agencies act essentially as advocates for private groups, there are many issues, especially in foreign policy, where "decisions are made by high public and private 'officials' in virtually a public opinion and interest-group opinion vacuum." [3] In areas of this sort, bureaucrats are in a commanding position to shape public policy by the weight of their own influence, since they possess not only the professional skills necessary to devise rational courses of action but also the ability to structure the public attitudes and preferences to which their policy decisions are in theory supposed to respond. In such situations executive agencies are not far from enjoying monopoly power over the course of public policy.

RESPONSIVENESS AND EFFECTIVENESS

The way in which executive agencies participate in policy-making — or what might be called the bureaucratic policy system — has traditionally been designed in terms of two criteria: The first is the responsiveness of the system — the extent to which it promotes a correspondence between the decisions of bureaucrats and the preferences of the community or the office-holders who are authorized to speak for the public. The second is the effectiveness of the system — the degree to which it leads to decisions that are more likely than alternative choices to bring about the outcomes that are desired, for, however laudable their goals, policies must work. Responsiveness and effectiveness are thus the touchstones by which we commonly measure the utility of a bureaucratic policy system.

At all levels of government in the United States, the task of creating acceptable arrangements to achieve these goals has been enormously complicated by the fact that the criteria of responsiveness and effectiveness often point in opposite directions. Organizational arrangements and procedures that appear perfectly designed to enhance the responsiveness of bureaucrats frequently seem less likely to allow them to produce effective decisions.

In national security administration, for example, the effectiveness of policy-making has usually seemed to demand a high degree of secrecy in bureaucratic deliberations. Apart from the obvious need to prevent disclosure of military or diplomatic information that might be helpful to a foreign adversary, the resort to secrecy in this area of policy has been justified on the grounds that it promotes candor in internal deliberations, and enables the government to gain the advantage of "surprise" in dealing with other states. The success of American policy in the Cuban missile crisis in 1962 has often been traced to the secrecy that surrounded the discussion within the government preceding the final decision to establish a blockade around Cuba.[4]

At the same time, however, the Cuban missile case highlights the fact that arrangements designed to enhance effectiveness in policy-making may clearly preclude the processes of popular consultation that are indispensable if responsiveness is to be secured. Certainly the kind of internal dialogue within bureaucracy that accompanied the Cuban crisis in 1962 could not have taken place in public while officials were considering alternative ways of dealing with the threat to American security that the Soviet missile bases then under construction appeared to represent. So decisions jeopardizing the survival of life on the planet were made by a handful of men acting in secret in Moscow and Washington.

There have been situations, of course, in which effectiveness and responsiveness in bureaucratic policy-making did not seem as incompatible as they did at the time of the confrontation with the Soviets in 1962. For example, after the invasion of Cuba by a refugee group supported by the United States had failed at the Bay of Pigs in 1961, President Kennedy conceded that the mistake of launching this attack might well have been avoided if there had been full disclosure of the plan to the American public and a broader discussion of it. Thus, in the case of the Bay of Pigs invasion it is possible that both the effectiveness and responsiveness of policy would have been better served by arrangements designed to promote public, rather than secret, decisions.

No president more devoutly advocated the necessity of secrecy for effective executive performance than President Nixon. In speaking before the American prisoners of war who had returned from Vietnam in 1973, Nixon was quite explicit in linking what he felt to be the great successes of his administration to the use of secrecy. "Had we not had secrecy," Nixon argued, "there would have been no China initiative, there would have been no limitation of arms for the Soviet Union and no summit, and had we not had . . . that kind of secrecy that allowed for the kind of exchange that is essential, you men would still be in Hanoi rather than Washington today."

Yet, it is one of the greater ironies of American history that this passion for secrecy was ultimately to prove the source of Nixon's undoing. His establishment of the so-called "plumbers unit" in the White House was motivated by a desire to maintain secrecy. The principal task of the plumbers was to plug up "leaks" of what the administration regarded as secret information, such as the earlier disclosure of the Pentagon papers, which had revealed much of the planning and discussions that took place in the executive branch in the early stages of the Vietnam War. After the ill-starred burglary of the national headquarters of the Democratic party by the plumbers, the White House made an immediate decision to "cover up" its connection with this covert operation. Thereafter the cover-up required an enormous and continuing investment in secrecy, culminating in the refusal to supply the tape recordings of White House conversations sought by the special prosecutor's office. The suspicion bred by each successive step in this continuing strategy of secrecy brought a precipitous decline in the president's standing in the eyes of both Congress and the public, and led ultimately to Nixon's departure from office under the threat of impeachment.[5]

The Watergate episode and other cases of its kind have led some observers to conclude that — from the point of view of effectiveness alone — the deliberations of executive officials should be as "open" as possible. Secrecy, it is argued, allows officials to cover up and continue ill-advised policies and to shield their own incompetence or misconduct from discovery. A system of disclosure, on the other hand, has a variety of practical advantages for the government as well as the public. For one thing it enables the president and other responsible executives to obtain better information on what is going on within the agencies they are supposed to supervise. Moreover, by widening the circle of those allowed to participate in executive discussions, an open system enables policy decisions to be informed by the advice and suggestions of many knowledgeable individuals who would otherwise be excluded from the deliberative process altogether.

Certainly, it is clear that there are a good many situations in which disclosure contributes to the effectiveness as well as the responsiveness of the policy-making process. It would greatly simplify the task of designing a bureaucratic policy system if this were the universal situation. Unfortunately, no such convenient correspondence between the requirements of responsiveness and the need for effectiveness can always be anticipated. While administrative arrangements designed to secure full publicity for all aspects of executive deliberations would help to prevent some mistakes in policy, they would also guarantee fewer successes. Not only in foreign affairs, such as the Cuban missile case previously cited, but also in domestic policy-making there are many situations in which the ability of executive agencies to carry on discussions in private while policies are being considered contributes to a thorough canvassing of all alternatives.

Consequently, it is not always possible to escape the difficult problem of devising arrangements that will help achieve quite contradictory goals. Gains in the effectiveness of the policy process may have to be paid for by some losses in its responsiveness, and it cannot always be assumed that measures designed to enhance responsiveness will not jeopardize the effectiveness of the system.

DESIGNING A POLICY SYSTEM

Even when there has been agreement on the need to maintain both effectiveness and responsiveness in the design of the bureaucratic policy system, there has not always been a meeting of minds on what each of these criteria requires. For some observers, responsiveness may simply entail the right of the public to determine what the ultimate objectives of bureaucratic activity shall be. By others it may be extended to include control by the public or its representatives of the day-to-day actions and decisions in which executive agencies engage in order to achieve these fundamental goals. It has long been argued whether legislatures should be confined to spelling out statutory guidelines for agency action, or encouraged in addition to monitor, as they often do, the ongoing decisions through which agencies pursue their statutory purposes.

Similar problems arise with respect to the distribution of authority in the bureaucratic policy system. In national administration, and at lower levels of government as well, responsiveness was long believed to require the centralization of authority in the hands of top executives. It was assumed that an executive at the commanding heights of an organization has the broadest of all perspectives on policy issues, and that he is most capable of focusing on the public interest. Officials at lower levels of administration, on the other hand, have traditionally been viewed as captive to more parochial concerns — the survival of their own unit or the needs of some special clientele, for example.

But what might be called a revisionist perspective in organization theory has acquired increasing strength in recent years. The argument is increasingly heard that responsiveness requires organizational arrangements under which a great deal of authority is delegated to lower levels of administration. Such decentralization, it is felt, "humanizes" bureaucracy because officials at the grass roots are more sensitive to the aspirations of the groups in the community immediately affected by the programs executive agencies are carrying out. Responsiveness is even better served, in the decentralist view, when the clients of executive organizations actually participate in official decision-making.

Effectiveness can be no less an ambiguous goal than responsiveness. Until recent times, concern over the effectiveness of the bureaucratic apparatus largely centered on the need to increase the ability of executives to control and direct the organizational units under their jurisdiction. Implicit in this approach was the assumption that the capacity of executive agencies to choose intelligent courses of action could be taken for granted. The problems of management were identified as essentially those of mobilizing the energy and resources of executive agencies toward the achievement of these agreed-upon goals. Increasingly, however, concern with the effectiveness in the bureaucratic policy system has come to center on the development of techniques for arriving at better decisions. Since it is now generally recognized that bureaucrats make, as well as carry out, policies, the quality of their decisions has become as important as the manner of their execution.

Thus, the institutional arrangements through which the goals of responsiveness and effectiveness are sought have tended to shift from one period to another. But the desire to achieve these not altogether consistent goals has been a constant objective from the first emergence of bureaucracy as an independent factor of major importance in American government in the late nineteenth and early twentieth centuries.

SCOPE OF THIS STUDY

Part one of this book focuses on the factors that account for the extraordinary influence bureaucrats now exert on policy decisions. Chapter two analyzes bureaucratic expertise and the way in which it manifests itself in the policy process. In all societies, whether democratic or undemocratic, modernized or less developed, executive agencies are rich repositories of specialized skills, and they can mold policy in many areas long before the public is even aware that any decisions need to be made. Chapter three deals with a special source of bureaucratic influence in democratic societies like the United States — the ability of executive agencies to build political support by mobilizing a constituency. Chapter four concludes this analysis of bureaucratic power with an examination of the factors that enable some agencies to have so much more influence on policy decisions than others.

In part two, the policy process itself is the central concern. Chapter five examines the internal politics of bureaucracy. Who are the principal participants in the decision-making process within executive agencies, and what impact does the bureaucratic environment itself have on policy outcomes? Chapter six presents an appraisal of current efforts to reform the way in which bureaucrats participate in policy-making. Particular attention is given in this connection to bureaucratic pathologies — the diseases that are said to afflict large organizations and make them ineffective as instruments for the achievement of policy goals.

In chapter seven, we return to the question that has been implicit throughout this discussion. Does the mounting influence of bureaucracy over all phases of policy in the modern state mean that a new power elite has emerged — controlling all decisions but itself uncontrolled? This is a key problem in every political system today, and it is of compelling importance in the politics of the newly emerging nations. Here bureaucratic power, particularly in the form of military organizations, is highly developed, while the governmental institutions through which this power can be offset, such as political parties and the judiciary, remain at a primitive stage of evolution.

This final chapter seeks to place bureaucrats in the context of the wider policy network with which they are linked — the system of executive politics in modern government — and to identify the circumstances in which bureaucratic power may be ascendant in the arena of national policy-making.

Notes

1. See, in this regard, the analysis of administrative activity as part of the group system of politics in David B. Truman, *The Governmental Process* (New York: Alfred A. Knopf, 1951), pp. 395–478, and Harmon Zeigler, *Interest Groups in American Society* (Englewood Cliffs, N.J.: Prentice-Hall, 1972), pp. 160–83.
2. Matthew Holden, Jr., " 'Imperialism' in Bureaucracy," *American Political Science Review* LX (December 1966): 951.
3. Theodore J. Lowi, "American Business, Public Policy, Case Studies and Political Theory," *World Politics* XVI (July 1964): 680.
4. For an analysis of the advantages and disadvantages of secrecy in the conduct of foreign affairs, see Thomas M. Franck and Edward Weisband, eds., *Secrecy and Foreign Policy* (New York: Oxford University Press, 1974).
5. For a fuller discussion of Nixon's orientation toward secrecy, see Francis E. Rourke, "Executive Fallibility: Presidential Management Styles," *Administration and Society* 6 (August 1974): 171–77.

Part One

THE SOURCES OF POWER

CHAPTER TWO

The Skills
of Bureaucracy

In all modern societies — whether democratic or nondemocratic — a first and fundamental source of power for bureaucratic organizations is the expertise they command — the fact that administrators bring to the policy process a wide variety of skills necessary both for making decisions on policy and for carrying out these decisions. This is what Max Weber long ago saw as the distinctive attribute that gave bureaucracy its enormous influence in modern government.

> The decisive reason for the advance of bureaucratic organization has always been its purely technical superiority over any other form of organization. The fully developed bureaucratic mechanism compares with other organizations exactly as does the machine with the nonmechanical modes of production. . . .
> Under normal conditions, the power position of a fully developed bureaucracy is always overtowering. The "political master" finds himself in a position of the "dilettante" who stands opposite the "expert," facing the trained official who stands within the management of administration.[1]

Such bureaucratic expertise is indispensable for the effective operation of any modern political system. The presence of bureaucrats in the governmental structure provides assurance that the decisions of political leaders will be guided by competent technical advice and carried out by skilled personnel. Moreover, in parliamentary political systems where the upper levels of political decision-making are not infrequently stymied by partisan strife, it is the experts in bureaucracy who take over and maintain the continuity of the government. No modern state could operate for a day without the performance of a myriad of tasks by highly trained bureaucracies.

The expertise of bureaucracy is no less important for the industrially backward nations. In these societies, modernization has required bureaucratization, and where administrative skills have been deficient, social and economic development have inevitably lagged.

But the autonomy that these bureaucratic skills generate is a source of widespread anxiety in all political systems, because of the possibility that administrative organizations will become "inner-directed" — responsive to cues and directions they give themselves rather than to those they receive from the political bodies that are the source of legitimate authority in the state. No fear has been more constant in modern politics — shared by revolutionaries and reactionaries alike — than the apprehension that bureaucrats might become a power elite and dominate the governmental process in which they are meant to play a subordinate role. The basic dilemma, as S. N. Eisenstadt puts it, is "whether bureaucracy is master or servant, an independent body or a tool, and, if a tool, whose interests it can be made to serve." [2]

THE ORIGINS OF BUREAUCRATIC EXPERTISE

There are a variety of ways in which public bureaucracies acquire the expertise that is so important an ingredient of their power in the governing process. For one thing, a large organization is itself a mechanism for enhancing human competence. People joined together in complex organizational systems can achieve results that individuals alone could never hope to accomplish — the construction of an atom bomb, the launching of a space vehicle into orbit, or the establishment of an educational system capable of meeting the intellectual needs of all citizens from primary school to post-doctoral training.

Organizations achieve this level of competence by taking complex problems and breaking them down into smaller and hence more manageable tasks. Once problems have been subfactored in this way, each segment can be handled separately, and then by piecing the parts together, an organization can provide solutions to what may have originally seemed to be insoluble problems. This division of labor within large-scale organizations also allows groups of employees to acquire specialized expertise, even though they may not themselves have unusual technical qualifications. It is for these reasons that an organization is itself a source of expertise, quite apart from the skills that its members initially bring to the job.

A second way in which bureaucracies acquire expertise is through the concentrated attention they give to specific problems. Dealing day in and day out with the same tasks gives public agencies an invaluable kind of practical knowledge that comes from experience. In time this knowledge becomes part of the memory of a government organization and is transmitted to new employees by training and indoctrination programs. The task an agency performs may not on the surface appear terribly complex — the cleaning of streets or the removal of snow, for example — but the agency is the institution in society that by experience has come to know the most about it.

The sustained attention that bureaucrats can devote to specific problems gives them a decided advantage over political officials who deal with a wide variety of problems and confront each issue of public policy only at sporadic intervals. This advantage is characteristic of both democratic and nondemocratic societies. It is perhaps particularly important in the United States because American bureaucrats tend to specialize early and to remain in the service of a particular agency throughout their career. But in European as well as American bureaucracies, expertise reflects continuity in office as well as concentration of energy. Not only do bureaucrats focus their attention on specific problems but they also remain in office for longer periods than is customary for politicians.

The knowledge that agencies acquire by continuous attention to particular functions puts them in an especially advantageous position to influence policy when the facts they gather cannot be subject to independent verification or disproof. Intelligence units are especially well situated in this respect. While it is not the only intelligence agency in the government, the CIA gathers and communicates data to the president that can heavily influence his decisions on foreign policy issues without his having any adequate assurance that the data on which he is acting belong in the realm of fact or fancy. Suppose, for instance, that "central intelligence were to report to the President that there was positive intelligence that the Soviet Union would attack the United States in forty-eight hours, how could he challenge the information? And the dilemma he would face would be particularly cruel because an enemy decision to attack can always be reversed, while a defensive action might, in some circumstances, itself provoke an attack." [3] A monopolistic or near monopolistic control of the "facts" thus provides tremendous reinforcement to the power that bureaucrats possess from specialized and continuous attention to a particular set of responsibilities.

But while organizations have certain inherent assets that contribute greatly to their decision-making skills, it is not these organizational characteristics alone that account for the expertise that is the hallmark of modern bureaucracy. In the modern state this expertise comes preeminently from the fact that a variety of highly trained elites practice their trade in public organizations — physicists, economists, engineers. In the roster of professions in American society there is not a single skill that does not find extensive employment in one or more executive agencies. And there are several professions such as the military that are employed only in the public service. Moreover, the tendency for professionals to seek employment in public as well as in private organizations is on the increase. Amitai Etzioni argues that as "the need for costly resources and auxiliary staff has grown, even the traditional professions face mounting pressures to transfer their work to organizational structures such as the hospital and the law firm." [4]

Of course, not all public organizations exhibit the same degree of professionalism in their employment pattern. Some administrative units like the U.S. Postal Service still hire mainly clerical employees. However, in other agencies, such as the National Institutes of Health (NIH), the level of professionalism is very high. Agencies like NIH are in fact often described as "professional organizations," since they are dominated by individuals whose primary commitment is to the skill they practice rather than to the institution by which they are employed.

Agencies that are highly professional in their orientation and employment patterns often occupy a preferred position within the structure of public bureaucracy. State universities, for example, are commonly conceded — by law or custom — a degree of administrative independence not allowed to other public agencies. The same tradition of autonomy ordinarily protects a research agency like the

Bureau of Standards from political pressures. When a professional agency enjoys such independence, the influence it exerts in all bargaining situations with other governmental units is greatly enhanced. In parts of the country where the standing of public higher education is at its peak, the state university has far more leverage than other agencies with the governor's office, the budget bureau, and legislative committees.

In the early history of American bureaucracy, such claims to expertise as administration could make were based largely on the factor of continuity — the clerical employees who then staffed government agencies worked so continuously on particular problems that they acquired a kind of specialized knowledge as an inevitable result. Their expertise had its genesis in their organizational position. And it exacted little deference from politicians. President Andrew Jackson's statement in this regard is often taken as the classic expression of popular disdain for the skills of bureaucracy in early nineteenth-century America: "The duties of all public officers are, or at least admit of being made, so plain and simple that men of intelligence may readily qualify themselves for their performance; and I can not but believe that more is lost by the long continuance of men in office than is generally gained by their experience." [5]

However, since Jackson's day there has been a sharp upgrading in the skills required to run the modern state. As the innovations wrought by science and technology have increasingly complicated both the environment and the responsibilities of government, the duties of the public service are no longer so "plain and simple" as Jackson once regarded them. Moreover, with the abolition of spoils and the increasing acceptance of merit as the essential qualification necessary for public employment there has been a growing effort to recruit experts to the public service, to provide in-service training programs designed to improve the skills of public employees once they are hired, and in a variety of other ways to encourage and enhance the development of bureaucratic expertise.

In summary, it can be said that bureaucratic expertise is rooted in both the characteristics of public organizations and, increasingly, in the skills of their members. Each year the operation of executive agencies at all levels of government demands the employment of a more diverse and complex range of specialized personnel. In sharp contrast to President Jackson's belief in the simplicity of the administrator's task stands the following statement by President John

F. Kennedy, delivered in support of an increase in pay for government employees: "The success of this Government, and thus the success of our Nation, depend in the last analysis on the quality of our career services. The legislation enacted by the Congress, as well as the decisions made by me and the Department and Agency heads, must all be implemented by the career men and women in the federal service. In foreign affairs, national defense, science and technology, and a host of other fields, they face unprecedented problems of unprecedented importance. We are all dependent on their sense of loyalty and responsibility as well as their competence and energy." [6]

EXPERTISE: CHANNELS OF INFLUENCE

Whether it stems from the characteristics of organizations or the skills of their members, bureaucratic expertise exercises influence over the development of public policy through three primary channels: (1) the ability of bureaucrats to give advice that often shapes the decisions of political officials; (2) the capacity of bureaucratic organizations to carry on the tasks that must be performed once policy goals are decided upon — the power of implementation; and (3) as a critical dimension of this power to implement policies, the discretion with which bureaucracies are commonly vested as they carry on the tasks of government.

In the case of advice, the power of bureaucrats is indirect, resting as it does upon their ability to persuade political officials that a certain course of action should be taken. Bureaucrats have influence only if politicians are willing to take their advice. However, once policies have been turned over to bureaucrats to implement, their power is direct. This is especially true when, as is common practice in all political systems, bureaucrats are granted the right to exercise discretion in the execution of policy. In such cases the actual content of policy may become predominantly a matter for bureaucratic determination.

ADVICE AS INFLUENCE

Nothing contributes more to bureaucratic power than the ability of career officials to mold the views of other participants in the policy process. Bureaucracies are highly organized information and advisory systems, and the data they analyze and transmit cannot help but influence the way elected officials perceive political issues and events. Herbert Simon has emphasized the importance of being able to shape the value or factual premises of decision-makers as a means of insuring control over decisions themselves, and it is precisely in this way that bureaucratic information and advice commonly function in the policy process.[7]

A notable illustration of the bureaucratic role in this respect was the influence exerted by George Kennan from his vantage point in the State Department in the years immediately following World War II. During this period, Kennan's arguments on the need to contain Soviet power and the methods by which this goal might be achieved did much to shape the assumptions on which American foreign policy was based in dealing with the Communist powers around the world. The views he expressed in a widely read article on foreign policy, which he wrote under the pseudonym of "X", became the basic American text of the Cold War for both government officials and attentive publics outside the government.[8]

The influence that bureaucrats exert on the policy process through their power to give advice should not be exaggerated. The American experience during the Cold War suggests that it is easiest for bureaucrats to appear powerful when their advice matches and reinforces the preexisting views of the political officials responsible for policy. As noted above, the advice of Kennan seemed highly influential in the early days of the Cold War, when the doctrine of containment was eminently congenial to the goals of leading political elites in the country. Later on, however, when Kennan attempted to restrain policy-makers from putting undue emphasis upon military force in applying the principle of containment, his advice was largely ignored, and he found himself increasingly isolated from power.[9]

Hence, the best way for a bureaucrat to acquire a reputation as the power behind the throne may be to confine himself to advice that fits in with the views of his political superiors, or to give advice only in areas in which he knows his superior has no very strong opinions. When Henry Kissinger served as special assistant for national security affairs during President Nixon's first term in office, he enjoyed a wide reputation as a highly influential advisor to the White House. But it is a fair assumption that Nixon initially chose Kissinger for this position because his views generally coincided with Nixon's own orientation toward foreign policy.

Kissinger's role could often have been that of reinforcing Nixon's capacity to pursue policies of his own choice, serving as an advocate or defender of the president's program with the National Security Council and the other executive agencies charged with responsibility for the conduct of foreign affairs.

But while the appearance and reality of bureaucratic power may not always coincide, it is clear that the ability to channel information into policy deliberations provides substantial leverage with which bureaucrats can affect the shape of decisions. If there are cases in which administrators appear only to be telling political officials what they want to hear, there are equally striking illustrations of situations in which staff members of executive agencies have substantially reshaped the attitudes of political leaders in both Congress and the executive. A notable example in this regard is the shift in the views of Clark Clifford on the Vietnam War following his appointment as secretary of defense in 1968. Clifford's transformation from a supporter to an opponent of American involvement in the war came about largely as a result of briefings he received from his civilian staff after he took over at the Pentagon. As a result of these briefings, Clifford himself became increasingly critical of the war in his advice to President Johnson, and helped push the president toward accepting the idea of a negotiated settlement.[10]

Advising the President. A group of agencies in which the power of advice can be seen in its most prominent form in American administration are the staff agencies that surround the presidency, administrative units like the Council of Economic Advisers or a scientific advisory committee. These agencies have little operational authority of their own. They influence policy primarily by influencing the president. The economists who serve with the Council of Economic Advisers can shape the president's perspective on fiscal policy, and hence his recommendations to Congress on tax and expenditure measures. Natural scientists who give advice to the president are equally influential with the chief executive in the areas of their scientific and technical competence.

The relationship between the president and his advisers at this level of administration involves reciprocal benefits: Through their role as bureaucratic advisors, professionally trained economists and natural scientists obtain a degree of influence in the policy process that they would never otherwise enjoy. The members of most professional groups have neither the time, inclination, nor the capacity to win political office, and involvement in bureaucracy is, therefore, the only avenue to political power open to them.

At the same time, however, the president also derives tangible political benefits from his use of experts. The wisdom of his policy decisions is greatly enhanced in the eyes of the electorate when it appears that these decisions rest on the best professional advice the White House has been able to obtain. As has been said, for example, of the Council of Economic Advisers: "The acceptance of the Council's expertise as the President's economists increases the acceptance of his authority in matters of economic policy, and where applicable it adds economic persuasion to his strategies of influence. In return, the President provides the principal market for the Council's expertise." [11] The same point has been made with respect to the role of natural scientists in government: "The scientist may find himself on the political firing line, placed there by a politician interested in using the scientist's prestige as an 'expert' to disarm the critics of his (the politician's) choices." [12]

There are risks as well as benefits for any political executive in his relationship with his advisers. It is, for example, highly important to a president that no one adviser be allowed to exercise monopolistic influence over his decisions. "An executive relying on a single information system became inevitably the prisoner of that system." So wrote Arthur Schlesinger, Jr., in describing the elaborate system of checks and balances that Franklin D. Roosevelt maintained to prevent any single adviser from becoming the Rasputin of his administration. "Roosevelt's persistent effort . . . was to check and balance information acquired through a myriad of private, informal, and unorthodox channels and espionage networks." [13]

The danger to which Schlesinger was pointing became abundantly clear during World War II when the Joint Chiefs of Staff began to exercise a high degree of influence over Roosevelt's decisions in the field of military affairs: "The mere fact of direct access to the President did not account for the authority of the Joint Chiefs in the conduct of the war. Their power was rather a product of their direct access combined with the exclusion of civilian advice. . . . Ironic as it was, Roosevelt, who normally skillfully played subordinates off against each other in order to maximize his own authority, allowed one set of advisers to preempt the field with respect to his most important decisions." [14]

One of the chief reasons why Roosevelt was not able to maintain the same balance with respect to military advice that he had earlier established in the domestic area was because military decisions had to be surrounded with so much more secrecy than domestic policy discussions. This requirement of secrecy prevented the use of an open system in which the president could draw advice from as many quarters as he chose: "Wartime . . . imposed secrecy and censorship. No longer could the President look anywhere and everywhere for scraps of information and advice on his preeminent concerns, his most compelling choices. No longer could he pick up any aide or friend he chose to spy out the terrain of his official advisers. His instinct for alternative sources, his avid curiosity, his reach for information and ideas, now had to be confined to men with a 'need to know.' " [15]

In domestic as well as military affairs, a president can overcome some of the disadvantages of dependence upon a closed circle of advisers by relying for advice upon committee structures that permit a broader canvassing of alternatives and even for the emergence of majority and minority points of view between which the president may choose. With a committee, a president has some assurance that the advice he is getting reflects pure expertise rather than — as might be the case with a single adviser — professional prejudice or personal idiosyncrasy. C. P. Snow's account of the excessive influence exercised over British Prime Minister Winston Churchill during World War II by his scientific adviser Lord Cherwell points up this problem. According to Snow, Churchill was led into serious mistakes in judgment through his dependence on Cherwell.[16]

In American government each of the major advisory institutions in the executive branch — such as the Joint Chiefs of Staff, the National Security Council, and the Council of Economic Advisers — is in fact a committee. In the literature of public administration, committees are usually held in low regard as instruments of management since they disperse rather than focus executive leadership and control. But as an advisory institution, the committee has a great deal of utility, and with administrative agencies moving increasingly into the development as well as the execution of policy, committees have become as indispensable for deliberative purposes in the administrative process as they have long been in legislative decision-making.

In recent years some presidents faced with the necessity of making critical decisions have set up high-level ad hoc committees to serve as advisory groups. Thus, in 1962 President Kennedy created the so-called Executive Committee of the National Security Council to weigh alternative strategies that the United States might pursue in countering the emplacement of Soviet missiles in Cuba. In 1968 President Johnson established a Senior Advisory Group to reevaluate American policy in Vietnam in the wake of the so-called Tet offensive by the Viet Cong and North Vietnamese troops. In each case these advisory committees included members drawn from outside the government, and their recommendations exerted strong influence upon ultimate presidential decisions.

From the perspective of the president or any agency head who uses any advisory body, such a group is most valuable if it is under his jurisdiction and owes its primary administrative loyalty to him. With this arrangement the executive has some assurance that advisers will look at problems from his perspective rather than from the vantage point of some institutional interest of their own. A model in this respect is the office of special assistant for national security affairs in the White House. This office has no constituency other than the president himself. It has no responsibility to Congress, since, under the doctrine of executive privilege, the special assistant for national security affairs does not have to testify before Congress unless he wants to. And it has no major bureaucratic interests of its own to advance or protect.

When the creation of a Council of Economic Advisers was first being considered in 1946, some congressmen tried to have it established as an independent agency responsible as much to Congress and the public as it was to the president. Their hope was that with independent status the agency would become a conservative influence upon the president, offsetting the influence exerted by liberal economists in his political entourage. This effort to create an independent council was not, however, successful, and the agency was set up as a staff arm of the presidency. To be sure, the first chairman of the council, Edwin Nourse, tried to maintain a position independent of the president, but council members since that time have defined their role as requiring administrative identification with the president. Their influence on policy has been chiefly a function of the president's willingness to call on them for advice.

Much the same evolutionary course was traced by the National Security Council (NSC), which was originally set up after World War II because Congress hoped to involve Cabinet officers in the conduct of foreign affairs. In the view of many legislators, Roosevelt's conduct of negotiations during World War II had been far too personalized, and they hoped that the NSC would become an inner cabinet which the President would be obliged to consult before making major national security decisions. However, President Truman, in whose term of office the NSC was established, made it clear very quickly that the NSC would meet and give him advice when and if he chose. Worth noting in this connection is the principle long ago enunciated by Machiavelli: "A wise prince, then, seeks advice continually, but when it suits him and not when it suits somebody else." [17]

Of course, an advisory group that is totally dependent upon the chief executive for its own survival may be highly reluctant to tell him unpleasant truths he ought to hear. In time, the advice a president gets from these experts may do little more than mirror his own opinions if advisers refrain from giving advice they perceive as going against the presidential grain. It may contribute to candor in the advisory process if advisers are drawn from universities or other outside institutions to which they can return if need be.

However, George Reedy argues that even members of the president's own staff, who generally come to the White House from outside the government, experience great difficulty in telling a president things that they believe he does not want to hear. As Reedy writes: "White House Councils are not debating matches in which ideas emerge from the heated exchanges of participants. . . . The first strong observations to attract the favor of the president become subconsciously the thoughts of everyone in the room." [18] Recognizing this tendency of advisory groups to defer to the chief executive, President Kennedy absented himself from the meetings of the NSC group charged with advising him during the Cuban missile crisis. But it is noteworthy that the strongest recommendations to come out of the NSC committee seemed to parallel closely proposals that Kennedy himself had initially favored.

To increase the likelihood that all alternatives will be canvassed before presidential decisions on foreign policy are made, Alexander George has proposed a system of "multiple advocacy" within the executive branch.[19] Under this arrangement the president would be obliged to intervene in the advisory process to make certain that important points of view are not being suppressed or ignored. In practice this has proven very difficult to do. Irving Janis contends that committees charged with making decisions have a seemingly irrepressible tendency toward what he calls "group think." According to Janis, there is a strain toward premature and erroneous consensus in committee decision-making — the members tend, whatever the diversity of their original views, to come together and reach agreement. The committee is not, therefore, a foolproof device for enabling a chief executive to escape the perils of the advisory process.[20]

Administrative Legislation. The impact of bureaucratic advice upon policy decisions stands out very clearly not only in the internal activities of the executive branch, but also in the deliberations of Congress on "agency bills" — legislation that has been originally drafted in the office of executive agencies. This administrative initiative in drawing up new legislation has not received much attention in recent years as was earlier the case.[21] Analysis of the origins of legislation has mainly focused on the increasing role of presidential leadership in the legislative process. Yet, this apparent presidential hegemony over Congress masks the fact that much of what ultimately comes to be regarded as the president's legislative program stems in the first instance from the advice of bureaucrats in the executive establishment. Located as they are in intimate contact with the everyday processes of government, bureaucrats have an unexcelled vantage point from which to see the need for new legislation. As Lawrence Chamberlain long ago pointed out in tracing the influence of bureaucracy on legislation: "The administrative officer lives with his job. In his daily concern with the raw material of administration, at the point where the government and the public meet, he becomes keenly conscious of the inadequacies, ambiguities, and lacunae of the law he administers." [22]

Of course, the role of executive agencies in actually originating legislation should not be exaggerated. Many bills drafted by bureaucrats have their inspiration outside of the executive branch altogether. These bills may be drawn up by executive agencies at the request of Congressmen, or constituency groups may seek an agency's sponsorship of legislative proposals designed to protect or advance their interests. Moreover, outside experts may be consulted or involved in the deliberations of executive agencies before the development of new legislation — as they were in the "task forces" employed by President Johnson to come up with new ideas for his administration.[23] But even when these factors are taken into account, the role of executive agencies in formulating legislation is still an extraordinary one. Robert S. Gilmour cites the case of the Department of Housing and Urban Development, which proposed "approximately 300 separate bills in the space of a single legislative year," and most of these were "initiated by the HUD bureaucracy." [24]

Modern presidents have sometimes regarded this bill-drafting activity of executive agencies as a threat to their own position of legislative leadership. This concern gave rise to the requirement that each agency clear its recommendations with the Bureau of the Budget (now Office of Management and Budget — OMB) before submitting them to Congress — a procedure designed to insure that these plans are in accord with the program of the president.[25] However, since the 1960s the White House staff no longer relies on OMB to protect the president's interests on major legislative proposals. Members of the staff have themselves begun to work jointly with departments that are developing legislation they regard as crucial. In the Nixon administration, this staff function was institutionalized in the Domestic Council, which was established to initiate and coordinate the legislative program of the executive branch.[26] Thus, the task of monitoring legislative proposals to make certain they are in accord with the president's program continues, but that function is increasingly performed by the White House staff rather than OMB. Structures change, but the function remains.

THE POWER OF IMPLEMENTATION

The expertise of bureaucratic organizations also manifests itself through control over the techniques by which policy is carried out and upon which its success eventually depends. While elected officials may have far-reaching ambitions for new programs or policies, the actual policy alternatives open to them in many situations are restricted to the courses of action their organizational machinery can carry out. Bureaucratic resistance or incapacity may spell the doom of even their most modest policy proposals.

Consider, for example, the case of an American president. There are many ways in which the enormous organizational apparatus over which he presides in the executive branch is an annoying burden to him. It often drags its feet in carrying out his proposals or generates jurisdictional disputes that he must settle — in this way consuming his time and exhausting his energy. But in the end the president is heavily dependent upon the ability of bureaucratic organizations for his own success. Indeed, as President Johnson discovered in the case of Vietnam, a president's orders may be disastrous for him if their execution is beyond the capabilities of his bureaucracy.

Graham Allison has given us an illuminating description of the degree to which the options open to political leaders are limited by the talents of the bureaucratic organizations under their jurisdiction. As Allison puts it:

> . . . existing organizational routines for employing present physical capabilities constitute the range of effective choice open to government leaders confronted with any problem. . . . The fact that fixed programs (equipment, men and routines that exist at the particular time) exhaust the range of buttons that leaders can push is not always perceived by these leaders. But in every case it is critical for an understanding of what is actually done.[27]

A telling illustration of Allison's argument was the role played by the development of a counterinsurgency capability in the American military apparatus. During the 1950s, one of the chief complaints leveled against the Eisenhower administration was the fact that it lacked the organizational capacity to conduct small-scale, limited wars. Because of this deficiency, it was argued, policymakers were forced to threaten nuclear war in situations in which it was not realistic to expect other countries to believe that this threat would ever be carried out. In the view of critics, this weakness in its military arsenal deprived American foreign policy of much of its capacity to deter undesired behavior on the part of adversaries in international politics.

When John Kennedy was elected president in 1960, one of the primary items on his agenda was the creation of a limited war capability that would end the nation's exclusive and ineffective reliance upon the nuclear deterrent and enable it to cope with what were believed to be Communist-led guerilla movements in the underdeveloped nations. The creation of this limited war capability under Kennedy made it possible for President Johnson to choose in 1965 to have American forces become directly and massively involved in ground combat in South Vietnam. In 1954, at an earlier stage of the war in Indo-China, when the United States had not yet developed such counterinsurgency techniques, President Eisenhower had refused to permit direct American participation in the war.

This is not to say that there is any iron law dictating that a bureaucratic capability once established will inevitably be used. But certain consequences do usually follow when an administrative organization is created to provide policy-makers with a desired capability. For one thing such an organization inevitably has a vested interest in its own survival. It will thus tend to search for missions through which its value to society can be demonstrated and the flow of resources into the organization encouraged. It thus stands to benefit from policies that enabled it to display its skills, and these policies acquire a weight in executive deliberations they would never otherwise possess.

Hence, a policy option that is strongly supported by an executive agency is much more likely to be adopted than one that lacks such sponsorship. Predicting which of several possible alternatives will be followed in the development of public policy can in no small measure be based on an assessment of the relative strength of the agencies responsible for carrying out each of the options under consideration. Policy-makers will always be under strong pressure to follow courses of action that serve strong organizational interests and to ignore those that do not. This is especially true in the area of national security affairs, where executive organizations play a large role in the development of national policy.[28]

Because bureaucratic organizations provide the capabilities through which policy decisions are executed, the actual shape of policy as it emerges from the machinery of bureaucracy reflects not only the intentions of decision-makers at the head of government, but also the characteristics of the organizations through which decisions are carried out. Policy outputs thus generate many surprises among political officials responsible for decisions, or what is often referred to as "unanticipated consequences." In extreme cases the original intention of policy-makers may hardly be visible in the outputs of the organization charged with putting decisions into effect.

Several characteristics of organizations help account for this tendency of organizational outcomes to diverge from original policy decisions. It is common for executive agencies to execute decisions through what organization manuals describe as standard operating procedures — predetermined ways of handling specific problems as they arise. These routines are the set procedures through which an organization has carried out its responsibilities in the past, and they have been sanctified by tradition and usually by successful experience. Employees have been programmed to perform these procedures and they are often subject to serious penalties if they deviate from them.

The ironic fact about such bureaucratic routines is that they are developed essentially to curb the ability of individual bureaucrats to influence policy through the exercise of personal discretion. Routines are designed to make the behavior of employees confirm to organizational goals rather than to their own personal inclinations. Organizations without routines make policy subject to the whims of individual bureaucrats. But while intended to limit the power of executive officials, such routines may also have the effect of enormously increasing the power of bureaucratic organizations in the total governmental process.

These bureaucratic routines derive much of their impact on policy from the fact that they are very difficult to start and, once begun, no less difficult to stop. Thus, the celebrated law of bureaucratic inertia: "bureaucracies at rest tend to stay at rest, and bureaucracies in motion tend to stay in motion." The slowness with which bureaucratic organizations respond to presidential desires for action is legendary and a constant source of exasperation for chief executives. It was not until six weeks after President Kennedy's Vienna meeting with Khrushchev that the State Department finally prepared a response to the Russian leader's *aide memoire* on Berlin.[29] Similarly, at the time of the Cuban missile crisis in October of 1962, Kennedy discovered that the American missiles he had ordered removed from Turkey several months earlier were still in place — a highly vulnerable target for Soviet efforts to win American concessions in exchange for removing Russian missiles from Cuba.

Exasperating as this inertia of bureaucratic organizations often is for American presidents, it is not altogether without value to them. The cumbersome routines through which bureaucratic organizations operate often save political officials from making an overly rapid or rash response in an emerging crisis. In 1969 an American reconnaissance plane was shot down by North Korea, and it was President Nixon's first inclination to launch a retaliatory air strike against North Korean airfields. He could not do so immediately, however, since it took considerable time for the American military apparatus to deploy the forces necessary to conduct such a mission. As it turned out, this delay provided Nixon with an opportunity to change his mind. "As the military slowly moved air and sea reinforcements toward Korea, his anger cooled and he decided against retaliatory raids." [30]

If the slowness with which executive agencies act in emergency situations can be described as a function of the inertia that characterizes large organizations, the difficulty of stopping bureaucratic organizations once they are launched upon a course of action reflects the momentum that bureaucratic routines acquire after being initiated. This momentum may take the form of carrying on procedures no longer needed simply because they have been built into an organization's repertoire, and their discontinuance would bring a reduction in the scope of an agency's activities or perhaps require the release of personnel. It may also reflect the fact that bureaucratic services generate constituencies that oppose their liquidation.

In 1970, for example, it was discovered that the army was still carrying on surveillance over civilian political activities that had been started during the period of civil disorders some years earlier to help the military subdue riots in several American cities. Once they were begun, these procedures proved very difficult to stop, mainly because other agencies of the government came to depend upon military intelligence for information on suspected subversives. "The intelligence operation generated a demand for its product from the Justice Department, the FBI, police departments and other government agencies. A source close to the operation said, 'We created addicts for this stuff all over the Government.' " [31]

In the cases just cited, bureaucratic momentum manifests itself in the ongoing performance of routines that are no longer required, since the problem to which they were addressed no longer exists. Such momentum may take the form of a series of logically progressive short-term decisions that escalate into consequences far beyond those originally intended. Some observers have interpreted the American involvement in Vietnam in precisely this way, as the final product of a series of continuing steps by bureaucratic organizations that were never intended to lead, as they ultimately did, into a major conflict. For example, the commitment of the air force to Vietnam to assist the South Vietnamese army led inescapably to the assignment of ground combat forces to protect the air bases that then became necessary, and the activities of such ground forces inevitably escalated from a simple protective role to "search and destroy" missions designed to forestall enemy attacks.

This tendency of bureaucratic momentum to transform small-scale commitments into large ones is highly visible in weapons development activities. Warner Schilling has shown that the original decision to enter upon the development of the hydrogen bomb was intended to leave open the possibility of discontinuing the project. However, once the H-bomb project was started, it required such formidable investments of resources over long periods that policymakers found themselves committed to the eventual production of the bomb as soon as they had decided to launch a preliminary inquiry to see if it was feasible to construct such a weapon.[32]

This kind of bureaucratic momentum tends to invalidate the argument of David Braybrooke and Charles E. Lindblom that policy-making in the United States is protected from irrationality by the fact that it moves incrementally in one sequential step after another from initial decision to final outcome, thus permitting a discontinuance of effort or the reversal of direction at any point at which either is considered desirable.[33] In actual fact the momentum of the organizations charged with putting a decision into effect may make it very difficult to stop or reverse gears once the bureaucratic machinery has been set in motion. Irreversibility may thus become a major hazard of policy decisions carried out through large organizations.

A chief factor contributing to such irreversibility is the fact that large bureaucracies arrive at policy positions only after an elaborate process of consultation and accommodation among diverse organizational interests. Agreements negotiated with such painstaking effort resist change, because such change would require reopening the whole bargaining process with no guarantee that the trade-offs required might not yield a less effective policy outcome.[34]

Recent years have seen increasing attention focused on these various problems of implementation — the difficulties that beset efforts to attain policy goals once they have been placed in the hands of bureaucracies. It has become much clearer than it once was that no policy decision should be finalized before the ease or difficulty of carrying it out has been taken into account, at least where the use of large-scale organizational processes is essential for the achievement of program objectives. In the past, the appraisal of policy alternatives has not always included the feasibility of implementation within the framework of analysis. This is what Graham Allison calls the "analysis gap" — the failure to study the area lying "between preferred solutions and the actual behavior of the government." [35]

This new interest in implementation contrasts sharply with the attention that management experts have traditionally focused on improving techniques for deciding on courses of action — systems analysis, cost-effectiveness ratios, and the other instruments of managerial science. It is now recognized that the most advanced techniques for making decisions are of little avail when no effective organizational procedures exist for translating these decisions into results. Jeffrey L. Pressman and Aaron Wildavsky have written a cogent study of the failure of a manpower training program in one American city, which they trace to the inadequate attention Washington gave to the obstacles implementation of this program would confront once it was established.[36]

THE EXERCISE OF DISCRETION

Control over the implementation of policy becomes especially important as a source of bureaucratic power when it includes the authority to exercise discretion in achieving policy goals. As used here, the term "discretion" refers to the ability of an administrator to choose among alternatives — to decide in effect how the policies of the government should be implemented in specific cases. The range of situations in which bureaucrats exercise discretion is virtually boundless. It includes the policeman deciding whether to make an arrest, a regulatory agency choosing either to issue or refuse a license or permit, or a public housing official evicting a tenant family on grounds of "undesirability." These decisions may have a vital effect upon the fortunes or even the fate of the individual concerned. Whether or not discretion is, as has been asserted, the "life blood" of administration, its exercise may certainly have a lethal effect upon the individual citizen. The capacity to exercise discretion in this way justifies Martin Shapiro's description of administrative agencies as "supplementary law-makers," functioning like courts to add on to the structure of the original legislation that Congress enacts through their own decisions and interpretations of statutes.[37]

In the traditional theory of public administration in the United States, it was assumed that the administrator's discretion extended only to decisions on means, while the ends or goals of administrative action were fixed by statute or by the directives of a responsible political official. This was the celebrated distinction between politics and administration presented by such early pioneers in the field as Woodrow Wilson and Frank J. Goodnow. This distinction was designed among other things to provide a rationale for insulating administrative agencies from exploitation by politicians bent on using administrative offices and powers as the "spoils" of victory at the polls. If bureaucrats did not shape policy, then there was no reason why administrative agencies could not be left in splendid isolation, free to make decisions on personnel, or on administrative organization and procedure, to attain maximum efficiency in carrying on the business of government. As Wilson puts it: "The broad plans of governmental action are not administrative; the detailed execution of such plans is administrative." [38]

This was a highly useful doctrine during the late nineteenth century and early twentieth century in the United States when public bureaucracy was an "infant industry" that needed a protective ideology behind which it could develop. It made the expansion of bureaucracy much less threatening to American democracy than it might otherwise have appeared to be. The doctrine cannot, however, be regarded as valid today when the center of power in policymaking has shifted from the legislative to the executive branch and when a great many bureaucratic decisions are recognized as having very large implications for policy.

The scope of this administrative discretion is vast in all societies with respect to both the everyday routine decisions of government agencies and the major innovative or trend-setting decisions of organizational life. These two broad types of administrative decision have been categorized by Herbert Simon as programmed and nonprogrammed decisions. In Simon's words: "Decisions are programmed to the extent that they are repetitive and routine, to the extent that a definite procedure has been worked out for handling them so that they don't have to be treated *de novo* each time they occur. . . . Decisions are non-programmed to the extent that they are novel, unstructured, and consequential." [39] Philip Selznick draws a parallel distinction between "routine" and "critical" decisions.[40]

The policy impact of administrative discretion when it is exercised with respect to nonprogrammed decisions is clear and unmistakable. If the Federal Reserve Board abruptly changes the discount rate, or alters the reserve requirements for member banks to control inflationary tendencies in a booming economy, or to stimulate investment in the face of an impending economic recession, these are major policy decisions of obvious importance to the society at large. Or the Federal Communications Commission when it sets forth criteria for determining how many television stations are to be allowed in each section of the country is obviously taking the lead in designing a national communications policy through the exercise of its discretionary authority. The independent regulatory agencies as a group have been assigned major responsibilities by Congress for making nonprogrammed decisions that require "a high degree of expertness, a mastery of technical detail, and continuity and stability of policy." [41]

What is perhaps not quite so clearly apparent is the power inherent in the capacity of bureaucrats to exercise discretion in the area of programmed or routine decision. The fact is, however, that decisions that may seem merely routine from the point of view of an administrative agency are often of critical importance to the parties affected by these administrative determinations. An individual denied the right to practice a profession as a result of a negative judgment on his or her qualifications by a licensing board has been grievously affected by the exercise of routine discretion in a situation in which the state controls entry into a profession. This penalty has been described as "professional decapitation."

Moreover, a government agency responsible for awarding defense contracts makes vital decisions for industries dependent upon these contracts for their survival, although the decisions may seem quite routine from the point of view of the agency. The exercise of discretion in an area of this kind has side-effects that reach far beyond the business firms immediately affected. The economy of an entire region may be heavily dependent upon the prosperity of a particular industry, and the denial of a defense contract or the closing of a military installation may represent an economic disaster for many communities.

The fact that routine administrative decisions can have such wide-ranging effects for individuals, private organizations, and local communities has led to the establishment of a variety of governmental arrangements designed to monitor these decisions. Individuals subject to the jurisdiction of regulatory agencies are, for example, commonly given an opportunity to appeal a decision adversely affecting their interests to a higher administrative authority. If this review does not lead to satisfactory results, there is in many cases an additional opportunity to obtain a judicial review of the administrative decision. Much of this review procedure rests upon statutory safeguards, such as the Administrative Procedure Act of 1946, or upon the due process requirements of state and national constitutions.

The judiciary is by no means the only outside institution that reviews administrative decisions. In certain areas of national administration Congress has also come to play an increasingly important role in overseeing the use of routine administrative discretion, although the fact that agencies have this discretion in the first place often springs from the fact that legislative mandates have been deliberately vague, passing on to the bureaucracy the responsibility for policy decisions. Congressional intervention in administration discretion is largely focused on the areas where large sums of money are involved, where the temptation to administrative corruption is great, and where the political side effects may be intense. Since 1964, for example, the secretary of defense has been obliged to give Congress thirty days' notice before closing any military installation.[42]

The president himself may find it expedient to monitor the exercise of bureaucratic discretion very closely when it is used in an area of critical national importance. During the war in Vietnam, for example, President Johnson personally participated in the selection of targets for American planes bombing in the North — a range of decision that in other wars was left to subordinate military officials. What this illustration suggests is that decisions which may in one set of circumstances be regarded as routine may in another context take on crucial importance.

In the Watergate affair President Nixon demonstrated that it may be equally advantageous for a president to maintain a certain distance between himself and the exercise of discretion by his underlings, if these subordinates are engaged in activities that are illegal or would embarrass the administration if they were disclosed. Watergate wove the concept of "deniability" into the national political vocabulary — an executive may find it useful to appear not to know about certain kinds of things. In the conventional wisdom at least such "deniability" is considered acceptable if it applies to the discretionary acts of American espionage agencies like the CIA abroad.[43] One of the many revealing aspects of Watergate was that it demonstrated how easily "dirty tricks" exported for use in the international arena could be imported back into domestic politics.

An administrative agency can itself go a long way toward controlling the decisions of its own employees through an effective program of internal training. In a study of the Forest Service, Herbert Kaufman showed how subordinate officials can be so thoroughly indoctrinated with policy goals that the exercise of their discretion can be relied upon to mirror faithfully the objectives of the organization. The premises on which their decisions rest have been firmly implanted by a uniform educational background, an effective program of in-service training, and an agency manual that clearly spells out the choices appropriate in particular situations.[44]

But even though there are manifold ways in which the use of discretion can be circumscribed and influenced by other participants in the policy process — political officials, judges, and nongovernmental groups — the power that accrues to administrative agencies because of their discretionary authority is still vast. Regulatory agencies, for example, exercise a great deal of power merely because they have the authority to give or withhold benefits, and to inflict or refrain from imposing sanctions. The fact that these agencies have such power forces a group subject to their jurisdiction to defer to them even in situations in which their actual legal authority may not be altogether clear. One of the most powerful sanctions a regulatory agency can impose upon a business firm is to publicize allegations detrimental to the product the firm is selling, even though subsequent investigation may show that these charges are not supported by the evidence.[45] While judicial review of administrative discretion may be theoretically available, its use in practice may be discouraged by many citizens' fear of suffering unpleasant publicity, or incurring the expense of legal fees, or simply the distraction and delay of litigation.

The history of the Central Intelligence Agency presents countless situations in which administrators have exercised discretion with far-reaching effects on the national welfare. The decision to send the ill-fated U-2 flight over the Soviet Union prior to the summit conference in 1960, the subsidies given to student and other nongovernmental groups in the 1950s and the 1960s, and the domestic spying activities of the agency revealed in the 1970s provide cogent examples of the ways in which discretionary authority vested in bureaucrats may come back to haunt responsible office-holders.

These illustrations should not, however, lead to the conclusion that the delegation of decision-making power to administrative agencies always has disadvantageous consequences. If this were actually the case, no such delegation would ever occur. The fact is, however, that the exercise of discretionary authority by administrators plays a vital role in protecting and advancing human welfare. Illustrations of these beneficial effects of discretion abound in the daily life of every American community, as public health officials inspect restaurants, fire departments enforce theater safety regulations, and the police attempt to control and prevent traffic accidents. Without administrative discretion, effective government would be impossible in the infinitely varied and rapidly changing environment of twentieth-century society. But the exercise of judgment involves choice, and choice means the formulation of policy. Hence, the high development of administrative discretion in modern society necessarily projects bureaucrats into the center of the policy process.

As many of the previous illustrations suggest, the use or misuse of administrative discretion has its greatest impact in the area of what Kenneth C. Davis has called "discretionary justice" — the use of discretion in ways that impact upon individual parties.[46] Discretionary justice is distinct from the general discretion administrators exercise in the development of public policy affecting classes of people or society as a whole. It arises in connection with innumerable programs that administrative agencies carry on that require a determination as to whether or not an individual party is entitled to a benefit, or should be subject to a penalty. "Street-corner" bureaucrats, particularly the police, play an especially important role in this respect. As Kenneth C. Davis puts it:

> Among the most important administrators in America are the police — all 420,000 of them. They make some of our most

crucial policies and a large portion of their function is the administration of justice to individual parties. . . . The police are constantly confronted with problems of fairness to individuals, and such problems are often intertwined with problems of policy. When should they not make an arrest that can be properly made? When should they stop and frisk? When should they say "break it up?" When should they make deals with known criminals, as with the addict-informer? What minor disputes should they mediate or even adjudicate? . . . These mixed problems of justice and policy are seldom decided by heads of departments but are left largely to the discretion of individual policemen.[47]

Studies have shown that individual policemen use the discretion thus placed in their hands in a wide variety of ways — depending on such factors as the nature of the policeman, the identity of the alleged offender, and the part of the country in which the law is being enforced.[48]

One point that should be borne in mind is that discretion can involve a great deal of anxiety for the person who exercises it as well as the private party subject to it. Not all bureaucrats enjoy using the power thus thrust upon them. Some retreat from discretion by citing the "rules" by which they are bound — an escape not usually open to police officers because of the absence of rules governing local law enforcement practices. An administrator with a sensitive conscience may be haunted by the possibility that an error in the use of discretion may have disastrous consequences for the persons subject to his or her authority.

Notes

1. H. H. Gerth and C. Wright Mills, *From Max Weber: Essays in Sociology* (New York: Oxford University Press, 1946), pp. 214, 232.
2. Samuel N. Eisenstadt, "Bureaucracy and Bureaucratization," in *Essays on Comparative Institutions* (New York: John Wiley & Sons, 1965), p. 179.
3. Harry Howe Ransom, *Can American Democracy Survive Cold War?* (Garden City, N.Y.: Doubleday Anchor Books, 1964), pp. 163–64.

4. Amitai Etzioni, *Modern Organizations* (Englewood Cliffs, N.J.: Prentice-Hall, 1964), p. 77. For a cogent analysis of the role of the professions in executive agencies, see Frederick C. Mosher, *Democracy and the Public Service* (New York: Oxford University Press, 1968), esp. pp. 99–133.

5. James D. Richardson, *Messages and Papers of the Presidents* (New York: Bureau of National Literature, 1897), III: 1012. For a full account of the origins of the Jacksonian attitude toward bureaucracy, see Matthew A. Crenson, *The Federal Machine: Beginnings of Bureaucracy in Jacksonian America* (Baltimore: The Johns Hopkins Press, 1975).

6. *Congressional Quarterly Almanac*, 1962, p. 907.

7. Herbert Simon, *Administrative Behavior*, 2nd ed. (New York: The Macmillan Co., 1957).

8. George F. Kennan, "The Sources of Soviet Conduct," *Foreign Affairs* 25 (July 1947): 566–82.

9. George F. Kennan, *Memoirs 1925–1950* (Boston: Little, Brown and Co., 1967), esp. pp. 354–67.

10. See Townsend Hoopes, *The Limits of Intervention* (New York: David McKay Co., 1969), pp. 151–224, and Patrick Anderson, *The Presidents' Men* (New York: Doubleday & Co., 1969), pp. 156–58.

11. Edward S. Flash, Jr., *Economic Advice and Presidential Leadership* (New York: Columbia University Press, 1965), pp. 309–10.

12. Warner R. Schilling, "Scientists, Foreign Policy, and Politics," in Robert Gilpin and Christopher Wright, eds., *Scientists and National Policy-Making* (New York: Columbia University Press, 1964), p. 169.

13. Arthur M. Schlesinger, Jr., *The Coming of the New Deal* (Boston: Houghton Mifflin Co., 1959), p. 523. However, Roosevelt took a number of major steps in domestic politics, including the decision to establish TVA and the court-packing scheme, without using the method of extensive prior consultation that Schlesinger attributes to him as a decision-making style.

14. Samuel P. Huntington, *The Soldier and the State* (Cambridge: Harvard University Press, 1957), p. 320.

15. Richard E. Neustadt, "Approaches to Staffing the Presidency: Notes on FDR and JFK," *American Political Science Review* 57 (December 1963): 859.

16. C. P. Snow, *Science and Government* (Cambridge: Harvard University Press, 1961). The Mentor edition, published in 1962 by the New American Library, has an excellent appendix on the Cherwell affair.

17. See *The Prince* in *Machiavelli, The Chief Works and Others*, trans. Allan Gilbert (Durham, N.C.: Duke University Press, 1965), I: 92.

18. George Reedy, *The Twilight of the Presidency* (New York: The World Publishing Co., 1970), p. 12.

19. Alexander M. George, "The Case for Multiple Advocacy in Making Foreign Policy," *American Political Science Review* 66 (September 1972): 751–85.

20. Irving L. Janis, *Victims of Groupthink* (Boston: Houghton Mifflin Co., 1972).

21. See, for example, *General Interim Report of the House Select Committee on Lobbying Activities*, 81st Cong., 2nd Sess., House Report No. 3138, Oct. 20, 1950, pp. 51–62.

22. Lawrence H. Chamberlain, *The President, Congress and Legislation* (New York: Columbia University Press, 1946), p. 24. For an early analysis of the administrator's role in framing legislation, see Edwin E. Witte, "The Preparation of Proposed Legislative Measures by Administrative Departments," in U.S. President's Committee on Administrative Management, *Report with Special Studies* (Washington, D.C.: U.S. Government Printing Office, 1937).

A more recent review may be found in Louis Fisher, *President and Congress* (New York: The Free Press, 1972), pp. 42–54.

23. See Norman C. Thomas and Harold L. Wolman, "The Presidency and Policy Formulation: The Task Force Device," *Public Administration Review* XXIX (September/October 1969): 459–71.

24. Robert S. Gilmour, "Central Legislative Clearance: A Revised Perspective," *Public Administration Review* XXXI (March/April 1971): 152.

25. See Richard E. Neustadt, "Presidency and Legislation: The Growth of Central Clearance," *American Political Science Review* XLVIII (September 1954): 641–71, and "Presidency and Legislation: Planning the President's Program," *American Political Science Review* XLIX (December 1955): 980–1021.

26. See Gilmour, "Central Legislative Clearance," pp. 156–58, and Fisher, *President and Congress*, pp. 52–54.

27. Graham T. Allison, *Essence of Decision: Explaining the Cuban Missile Crisis* (Boston: Little, Brown and Co., 1971), p. 79.

28. See the discussion of this point in chapter three, pp. 72–75.

29. Arthur M. Schlesinger, Jr., *A Thousand Days* (Boston: Houghton Mifflin Co., 1965), p. 384.

30. *The New York Times*, January 21, 1971, p. 12.

31. Ibid., January 18, 1971, p. 22.

32. Warner Schilling, "The H-Bomb Decision: How to Decide Without Actually Choosing," *Political Science Quarterly* 76 (March 1961): 241–46.

33. David Braybrooke and Charles E. Lindblom, *A Strategy of Decision* (New York: Free Press of Glencoe, 1963).

34. See in this connection, Henry A. Kissinger, *American Foreign Policy* (New York: W.W. Norton & Co., 1969), p. 20.

35. Graham Allison, *Essence of Decision*, p. 267. For a thorough analysis of this implementation problem, see Erwin C. Hargrove, *The Missing Link: The Study of the Implementation of Social Policy* (Washington, D.C.: The Urban Institute, 1975).

36. Jeffrey L. Pressman and Aaron Wildavsky, *Implementation* (Berkeley: University of California Press, 1973).

37. Martin Shapiro, *The Supreme Court and Administrative Agencies* (New York: The Free Press, 1968).

38. Woodrow Wilson, "The Study of Administration," *Political Science Quarterly* II (June 1887): 212. The origins and development of this essay are traced in Richard J. Stillman, II, "Woodrow Wilson and the Study of Administration: A New Look at an Old Essay," *American Political Science Review* LXVII (June 1973): 582–88.

39. Herbert A. Simon, *The New Science of Management Decision* (New York: Harper & Row, 1960), pp. 5–6.

40. Philip Selznick, *Leadership in Administration* (Evanston, Ill.: Row, Peterson & Co., 1957), pp. 29–64.

41. Marver H. Bernstein, *Regulating Business by Independent Commission* (Princeton, N.J.: Princeton University Press, 1955), p. 4. See also Louis M. Kohlmeier, *The Regulators* (New York: Harper and Row, 1969).

42. For an analysis of legislative review of administrative decisions, see Joseph P. Harris, *Congressional Control of Administration* (New York: Doubleday Anchor Books, 1965), pp. 226–76.

43. President Dwight D. Eisenhower was widely criticized in 1960 when he revealed personal knowledge of and assumed responsibility for an unsuccessful U-2 spy flight over the Soviet Union. High officials are considered to have

the discretion to lie in dealing with foreign adversaries. See David Wise, *The Politics of Lying* (New York: Random House, 1973). As Wise shows, however, these officials can use this discretion by pretending to lie to enemies abroad in order to lie to their own people.

44. Herbert Kaufman, *The Forest Ranger* (Baltimore: The Johns Hopkins Press, 1960).
45. For some graphic illustrations of this unwarranted use of publicity as a punishment see Ernest Gellhorn, "Adverse Publicity by Administrative Agencies," *Harvard Law Review* 86 (June 1973): 1380–1441.
46. Kenneth C. Davis, *Discretionary Justice* (Baton Rouge: Louisiana State University Press, 1969).
47. Ibid., p. 8.
48. Among the best of these studies are Jerome Skolnick, *Justice Without Trial* (New York: John Wiley & Sons, 1966) and James Q. Wilson, *Varieties of Police Behavior* (Cambridge: Harvard University Press, 1968).

CHAPTER THREE

The Mobilization
of Political
Support

In an open system of politics, a vital source of power for administrative agencies is their ability to attract the support of outside groups. Strength in a constituency is no less an asset for an American administrator than it is for a politician, and some agencies have succeeded in building outside support as formidable as that of any political organization. The lack of such support severely circumscribes the ability of an agency to achieve its goals, and may even threaten its survival as an organization. As Norton Long puts it: "The bureaucracy under the American political system has a large share of responsibility for the public promotion of policy and even more in organizing the political basis for its survival and growth." [1]

This entanglement with politics has been a characteristic of American administration since at least the days of President Andrew Jackson. The intrusions of politics came first from the political parties, anxious to use administrative jobs as building blocks in the construction of party organizations. However, beginning with the Pendleton Act in 1883 that established the Civil Service Commission, the ability of political parties to exploit administrative agencies in this way was increasingly subject to legal restriction. Slowly but surely, the principle came to be accepted that appointments to career positions in the public service should go to those who are technically qualified without regard to their party affiliation. [2]

But this development by no means banished politics from American administration. Since American political parties did not always function effectively as organizations for the development and support of policy objectives, administrative agencies were forced to develop their own basis of political support, negotiating alliances in and out of government with a variety of groups that could be used to advance bureaucratic objectives or to assist an agency in fending off attack. The political neutralization of bureaucracy is impossible in a country in which the political parties are incapable of performing the functions expected of them in the governmental structure of which they are a part. When the parties do not provide for program development and the mobilization of political support, executive agencies must perform these tasks for themselves, or seek support from outside groups that will help them do so. Noteworthy here is the fact that legislation like the Pendleton Act excluded political parties from intervening in the affairs of executive agencies but left other political organizations such as interest groups free to become involved in agency decision-making.

From the point of view of an administrative agency, there are three vital centers from which political support may be drawn: the outside community, the legislature, and the executive branch itself. All these sources of political strength may be cultivated simultaneously, and usually are; or one may be nursed virtually to the exclusion of the others. The possibility of choice often calls for the exercise of administrative statecraft of a high order to balance one source of strength against another, in this way building an enclave of political independence. Sometimes, however, no choice is possible. A state treasurer directly elected by the legislature cannot easily look elsewhere for political support. An executive budget office is, in most circumstances, politically captive to the chief executive it serves. If he does not choose to give it political standing, then it has none. These and other possibilities are examined in the pages that follow, as each of the various ways in which administrative agencies build political support is examined in turn.

BUREAUCRACY AND ITS PUBLICS

Basic to any agency's political standing in the American system of government is the support of public opinion. If it has that, an agency can ordinarily expect to be strong in the legislative and the executive branch as well. Since public opinion is ultimately the only legitimate sovereign in a democratic society, an agency that seeks first a high standing with the public can reasonably expect to have all other things added to it in the way of legislative and executive support. Power gives power, in administration as elsewhere, and once an agency has established a secure base with the public, it cannot easily be trifled with by political officials in either the legislative or executive branch.

Attentive and Mass Publics. There are essentially two ways in which public support may be cultivated. The first is by creating a favorable attitude toward the agency in the public at large. The second is by building strength with "attentive" publics — groups that have a salient interest in the agency — usually because it has either the capacity to provide them with some significant benefit, or the power to exercise regulatory authority in ways that may be of critical importance to the groups concerned.

These methods are not mutually exclusive. An agency can seek to create general public support while assiduously building alliances with interest groups that have a special stake in its work. This is in fact the strategy most agencies follow, to the extent that is available to them. Actually, only a comparatively few agencies carry on functions that have a high degree of visibility for the general public. An agency like the FBI, which has been performing a dramatic role in American life for several decades, does command a broad pattern of public support that stretches throughout all strata of society. Part of this public standing may be said to spring from skillful use of publicity — agencies like the FBI exploit every opportunity to catch the public eye with their achievements. But the power of publicity is not boundless, even in America where good public relations are a first concern of every large organization, and an agency whose activities do not match the FBI's in intrinsic dramatic appeal will not equal it in public esteem no matter how assiduously it carries on public relations activity.[3]

There may be occasions, of course, when any agency may find itself basking temporarily in the limelight of publicity. The Food and Drug Administration, for example, may languish out of sight as far as the general public is concerned, until suddenly the injurious effects of a new drug arouse public concern, as was the case a few years ago with thalidomide, a tranquilizer whose use by pregnant women brought about the delivery of a large number of infants with birth deformities. Immediately, the agency and its pronouncements became a matter of front-page interest. For a brief period at least, it was an organization with a very extensive public indeed. Or, a state air pollution commission, conducting its affairs in almost 'total obscurity, may suddenly find itself projected to the forefront of public attention by the onset of severe atmospheric smog. In a case of this kind, the head of such an agency may find himself an overnight celebrity.

What these illustrations suggest is the fact that many agencies have a potential public that far exceeds the size of their normal clientele. The existence of such a potential public reflects the fact that an agency carries on activities that affect the interests of a far larger group than the public which consistently identifies itself with its program. Both the food and drug and air pollution agencies are in the public health field, where agencies perform functions that are of vital importance to a general public that may not even be aware of their existence. However, if events arouse the attention of a latent public, as the environmental and energy crises have done in recent years, an agency's image in the community and the legislature may suddenly swell in importance. To the extent that it is affected by shifts in the general climate of public opinion, administrative power may thus be extremely volatile, shifting — like a politician's — with changing tides of public sentiment, or what Anthony Downs calls the "issue-attention cycle." [4]

It should not be overlooked that any sudden expansion in the size of the public that takes an interest in its activities may impact on an agency as a threat rather than an opportunity. Its new following may include groups of organizations that are extremely suspicious of the way in which the agency has been carrying on its activities in the past. The agency may thus come under a critical scrutiny it never before experienced, and it may soon find itself under strong pressure to change the thrust of its decisions. E. E. Schattschneider has emphasized that the outcome of the policy deliberations in which governmental actors engage can be altered by shifts in the size and character of the audience before which these deliberations take place.[5] A forestry agency, for example, may find that decisions on the use of public lands in harvesting timber that were quite acceptable to the lumber industry with which it has long worked are highly repugnant to environmentalists who move into the agency's constituency.

Moreover, a study by Charles Jones of the national air pollution agency showed that a sudden and substantial expansion in the size of the public that supports what an agency is doing may also represent a threat to it.[6] Between 1965 and 1970 the number of people concerned about air pollution jumped markedly, and these new constituents expected the national agency to do much more to solve the pollution problem than it was capable of doing. Great expectations can thus be as threatening to an agency as indifference on the part of the public, if these expectations seem likely to be disappointed and subsequently converted into hostility.

Hence, it is essential to every agency's power position to have the support of attentive groups whose attachment is grounded on an enduring tie. The groups an agency provides tangible benefits to are the most natural basis of such political support, and it is with these interest groups that agencies ordinarily establish the firmest alliances. Such groups have often been responsible for the establishment of the agency in the first place. Thereafter, the agency and the group are bound together by deeply rooted ties that may be economic, political, or social in character. From an economic perspective, the agency usually carries on activities that advance the material welfare of members of the group. The group in turn may supply private employment opportunities for employees of the agency. Also, in return for the political representation with which the agency provides the group in the executive apparatus, the group ordinarily supports the agency in a variety of its own political undertakings, including its requests for financial support, its attempts to secure the passage of legislation expanding its powers, or its efforts to defend itself against legislative proposals that threaten its administrative status. Finally, frequent social contact between agency and group breeds ties of familiarity and friendship that help seal the alliance. In its most developed form the relationship between an interest group and an administrative agency is so close that it is difficult to know where the group leaves off and the agency begins.

This identity between an interest group and an executive agency is strongly reinforced by the practice, especially common at the state level, of having occupational or professional qualifications as a requirement for appointment to administrative office. Under law, the members of a state real estate commission may have to be licensed real estate brokers, and similar requirements often prevail with respect to other administrative boards having the power of occupational licensing in the states. In fields such as law or medicine, the state may virtually turn over a licensing agency to its professional constituency — to be used at the group's discretion for its own purposes.

Such arrangements merely give formal legal blessing to the common political practice of allowing interest groups to have a major voice in, if not a veto power over, appointments to agencies that administer functions in which they have a vital stake. Legal support for interest group involvement in the affairs of administrative agencies may also come from statutes requiring group representation on agency advisory committees, or stipulating, as is common, for example, in agricultural administration, that the agency secure the consent of interest group members before exercising certain regulatory powers. There are also cases — the administration of grazing on public lands in the West, for example — where individuals representative of interest groups are given the power to enforce administration regulations at the point of impact.[7]

Organizing a Clientele. Agencies that are not in a position to dispense important benefits or favors that are of substantial value to any segment of the community are in a disadvantageous position with respect to their ability to attract organized group support. The State Department is commonly regarded as having no "natural constituency" in the sense of clientele groups for which the department is able to do tangible and significant favors. Even though the fate of the entire population may depend on the effective conduct of foreign affairs, there is no strongly organized group structure in the outside community that regards the department as "its department," and stands ready to defend and assist it in attaining its goals.

However, even the State Department has been able to identify a large number of groups with which it maintains close liaison on foreign policy matters.[8] And some of these groups can play a significant role in the conduct of foreign affairs. For example, the International Longshoreman's Association has periodically refused to load commodities like wheat on ships destined for the Soviet Union and other Communist countries. For many of these outside organizations, however, the work of the department is of secondary rather than primary importance. Their interest in foreign affairs is something less than an intense preoccupation.

Hence, in order to secure public backing on matters of major concern to it, the department has often had to resort to organizing outside group support itself. If the mountain will not come to Mahomet, Mahomet will go to the mountain. The organization by the department of a blue-ribbon committee of distinguished citizens to lead a campaign in behalf of the Marshall Plan in 1947 is an illustration of the department's success in establishing its own public support,[9] and this kind of stratagem has been used by the department to accomplish a variety of other foreign policy objectives. For example, a committee of prominent citizens was organized to support President Johnson's policies during the Vietnam War and was given the title of Citizens Committee for Peace with Freedom in Vietnam.

But the truth of the matter is that, while agencies in the field of national security affairs give a good deal of lip service to the idea of consulting with the public, in actual practice this consultation commonly consists of getting groups of citizens together so that they can be indoctrinated with the official point of view. These national security agencies are much better at transmitting than they are at receiving messages from the public. Viewing themselves as having the best information available on the issues with which they deal, they communicate with the public not for the purpose of obtaining feedback that will be useful in shaping policy, but in order to structure public opinion so as to make it more supportive of their policies, or to prevent opposition from developing.

Executive agencies like the State Department can also be extremely adroit in organizing pressures upon themselves to which they seem to be responding, but which they are in fact initiating. The organization of such apparent pressure group activity thus provides a means by which these agencies can conceal their own central role in the policy process. The initiative appears to be with outside organizations, but the activities of these external groups are actually instigated by the agency itself. Of course, one risk an agency runs in following this strategy is that the mass opinion it is helping to create may eventually be a constraint upon it when and if it decides to change the policies for which it is currently seeking public support.

Domestic agencies have been even more adept at organizing their own infrastructure of interest group support. The Department of

Agriculture played a principal role in the organization and development of the American Farm Bureau Federation — the largest and most powerful of the agricultural interest group organizations.[10] And very early in its history the Department of Labor became convinced that the only way in which it could reach the wage-earning clientele it was obligated to serve was by encouraging the development of trade unions. Labor organizations provided an avenue for the dissemination of the informational material that was, in the beginning, the department's chief contribution to improvement of the welfare of its wage-earner clientele. The department had to communicate with its constituency, and, as it was to point out itself: "Freely as conferences with unorganized wage earners are welcome, official intercourse with individuals as such has practical limits which organization alone can remove."

Not only did the department thus defend its close liaison with existing trade union organizations; it also came, not illogically in view of the need to facilitate communication with its clientele, to support the extension of trade union organization among wage earners. The reason the department gave for this support was that the growth of labor union membership would facilitate collective bargaining and promote industrial peace. "The absence of organization," the department stated, "means the absence of a medium through which the workers en masse can discuss their problems with employers. The denial of this organization is the denial of the only means of peaceable settlement they have." Of course, pragmatic considerations were also involved in the department's support of expanded trade unionism, such as the fact that the strengthening of wage-earner organizations would increase the size of the department's effective clientele and the weight of its political support.[11]

Perhaps the worst hazard an agency faces, when it deliberately sets out to establish an infrastructure of interest group support, is the possibility that, once established, these groups may break away from agency control, or even become a focus of opposition to it. The parent-teacher associations set up in conjunction with school systems at the local level generally play a useful role in providing citizen support for the education officials. But if these PTA organizations are captured by opponents of the existing educational system, as has occurred in some areas, then they provide a formidable vehicle for mobilizing opposition to school administrators — more effective, because of their organizational capability and semiofficial status, than any other resource at the disposal of critics of the educational establishment.

One of the major advantages that the support of interest groups has for an executive department is the fact that such groups can often do for a department things that it cannot very easily do for itself. In national politics, for example, interest groups can take a position on policy questions that department officials secretly hold but cannot publicly advocate because it may put them in disfavor with the president. The outside groups that support each of the various branches of the armed forces in the Department of Defense have often given military officials assistance in precisely this way. As Samuel P. Huntington puts it:

> The allies and supporters of a service are at times more royalist than the king. They do not necessarily identify more intensely with service interests than do the members of the service, but they do have a greater freedom to articulate those interests and to promote them through a wider variety of political means.[12]

While deference to their commander-in-chief may not permit military officials to disagree openly with the president when he cuts their appropriation or gives another service jurisdiction over a weapons system they believe to be rightfully theirs, no such restrictions prevent defense industries with which they have contractual relations from springing to their defense, or keep a back-stop association, such as the Navy League and the Air Force Association, from vociferous protest against efforts to trim the appropriations or the jurisdiction of a military agency.

Outside organizations thus play a valuable role in enabling administrative agencies to oppose directives from the chief executive. They are also useful in helping these agencies evade legislative controls. Congress has enacted statutes designed to prevent administrative agencies from propagandizing the public in their own behalf, or lobbying in the legislature to secure the passage of bills they favor. These laws are difficult to enforce, since administrative agencies are also charged with responsibility for keeping the public informed on what they are doing, and the line between unlawful propaganda and legitimate public information activity is as fine as any distinction that exists in the American political system. But agencies can escape these restrictions in any case by having outside organizations carry on such public relations or lobbying activity for them. Senator Barry Goldwater of Arizona once observed that "the aircraft industry has probably done more to promote the Air Force than the Air Force has done itself." [13] This kind of claim could be made for a great variety of interest groups that identify and associate themselves with the fortunes of an executive agency.

There are other intermediaries bureaucratic organizations can use in their efforts to shape public opinion. Agencies will often give information they want disclosed to a sympathetic congressman and rely on him to perform the task of disseminating it to the public at large. The transmission of information in this way represents a profitable exchange for both parties. The congressman attracts public attention to himself and enhances his own career by generating news. The executive organization gets its message across to the public and in the process ties a congressional supporter even more firmly to its own cause, since he has benefitted from his role as intermediary for the organization. Members of the Armed Services Committee in both the House and the Senate have often served their own and the Pentagon's purposes in precisely this fashion.

A friendly news media representative can perform the same function. An agency can "leak" information to a reporter or allow him to identify it as coming from "anonymous" or "highly placed" sources in the agency. Again the transaction is one that serves the interests of both the giver and the receiver of information. The agency succeeds in getting information disseminated to the public and the reporter or columnist obtains a highly prized exclusive story. Such relationships between secretive agencies like the CIA and friendly newspaper columnists are not uncommon in the United States.[14] An agency that has secrecy as one of its distinguishing characteristics is in an advantageous position to give a reporter preferred access to a story.

The Captive Agency. The help it receives from interest groups is not without its perils for an administrative agency. The agency may come to lean so heavily on the political support of an outside group that the group in time acquires a veto power over many of the agency's major decisions. In extreme cases of this kind, the agency becomes in effect a "captive" organization — unable to move in any direction except those permitted it by the group upon which it is politically dependent.

Administrative units that are especially vulnerable to domination of this sort are clientele agencies — public organizations established to provide comprehensive services to a special segment of the population. On the national scene such clientele agencies include the Veterans Administration, the Department of Agriculture, the Children's Bureau, and the Department of Labor. Each of these agencies has a long history of close association with and subordination to outside organizations representative of its clientele.

As noted earlier, the Department of Labor was from its very beginning closely identified with the trade union movement. When it was first set up in 1913, the department was, as Samuel Gompers put it, intended to be "Labor's Voice in the Cabinet." While this relationship was helpful in many ways, it also tended to narrow the scope of the department's authority. For one thing, the trade unions were allowed to exercise a great deal of influence over major department decisions — including the selection of assistant secretaries of labor. In addition, this association with the union movement made the department suspect in the eyes of other groups — employers, for example — and for a long time its jurisdiction over labor activities was limited by the reluctance of business and agricultural groups to allow the department to administer functions where its bias in favor of the trade unions might be disadvantageous to their interests. As this illustration makes clear, an agency makes enemies as well as friends when it identifies itself with a particular population group, since it inherits hostilities directed at the group with which it has entered into an alliance.

The submissive posture of a clientele agency toward its constituency is not, of course, a permanent genuflection. During the Eisenhower administration, for example, the assistant secretaries of labor were not chosen by the trade unions. As compared with other periods in its history, the Veterans Administration displayed a great deal of independence from the veterans groups with which it is allied when it was headed by General Omar Bradley — a career officer with a distinguished record in World War II. Leadership by a vigorous personality may thus uncover latitude for independent action by an executive agency that previously had not been thought possible.

The tendency of clientele agencies to fall under the control of the groups they serve has often been used as an argument against organizing the executive branch upon the basis of the clientele principle. The contention is made that executive agencies can be prevented from becoming the tools of political groups only if administrative tasks are divided on the basis of some other principle of organizational design. But, in point of fact, it is difficult to identify a principle of organization that will not engender a very close relationship between an administrative agency and the groups that benefit from the activities it carries on. In terms of classical organization theory, the principal alternatives to clientele as a basis for allocating tasks among administrative agencies are the criteria of function to be performed, process or skill to be carried on by agency personnel, or geographical area to be served. However, agencies organized on the basis of function, such as highway, welfare, or education departments, are also susceptible to domination by outside groups, as are agencies organized on the process or skill criterion — the Corps of Engineers, for example.

As far as organization in terms of area is concerned, Philip Selznick's classic study of the interaction between a public agency and its environment — *TVA and the Grass Roots* [15] — clearly revealed a pervasive pattern of outside control over the foremost agency of the national government organized on the basis of geographical area, the Tennessee Valley Authority. In return for the support it received from important groups in the Valley area, the TVA proceeded to modify many of the original objectives of its agricultural program that were offensive to this constituency.

Of course, in its own defense, the agency could point out that the goals it modified were not of salient importance to it, that its real concern was with its public power program in the Tennessee Valley, and if support for this activity could only be obtained by "selling out," so to speak, on agricultural goals, then this was an exchange well worth making. Selznick himself later conceded the validity of such a strategy:

> . . . the TVA purchased a considerable advantage with these concessions. It gained the support of important local interests and of a powerful national lobby. These defended not only the agricultural program but TVA as a whole. In this way, by modifying its agricultural program and certain broad social policies, the Authority was able to ward off threatened dis-

memberment and to gain time for the successful development
of its key activity — the expansion of electric power facilities.[16]

Any public agency may thus find it necessary to yield control over
a segment of its program to a significant interest group in order to
buy the support of that group for more important policy goals. A
state university, for example, may tailor its program of agricultural
education to fit the needs of important farm groups, so as to obtain
the support, or at least neutralize the opposition of rural groups to
other educational activities in which the university may wish to
engage. Some of an agency's activities may thus serve as "loss leaders" — activities that represent a loss or at least small profit from
the point of view of an agency's major goals, but that simultaneously widen the basis of political support for objectives that are of
more significance to it. In the case of a state university again, its
intercollegiate football program may represent just such a "loss
leader." The support engendered by the achievements of its football team may quicken the allegiance of alumni and other citizen
groups to the university in areas of science and culture far removed
from the gridiron.

There is always the possibility that this kind of support will be
purchased at the price of serious damage to major institutional
goals. Activities that are initially designed to be merely supportive
in character may in time grow so large as to have wide-ranging and
debilitating effects upon an institution's capacity to achieve its
major goals. In the case of the state university, for example, its agricultural school may dominate the image a university radiates to the
outside world, and this reputation as a "cow college" may seriously
handicap its ability to attract faculty and students for nonagricul-
tural programs. Or a football program established to win support
for academic activities may eventually lead to a serious dilution in
educational quality as standards are lowered in order to recruit
athletic talent.

Goal distortion of a serious kind is thus always a possible price
of constituency support. The worst illustrations of this have occurred in the area of regulatory administration. At both the state
and national level of government, agencies established to regulate
particular kinds of economic activity have always exhibited an extraordinary penchant for falling under the control of the groups
placed under their jurisdiction. The regulatory agency thus be-

comes in effect the pawn of the regulated industry. This kind of relationship represents a radical inversion of organizational goals, as an agency enters into collusion with the very group whose behavior it is supposed to control.[17]

While it is easy to censure this kind of collusion, a close relationship between a regulatory agency and the groups under its jurisdiction is often essential to an agency's achievement of its goals. In the case of an air pollution commission, for example, the effectiveness of the commission may be enormously enhanced by including in its membership representatives of some of the principal industries responsible for the discharge of waste materials into the atmosphere. These representatives can help secure the compliance of their firms with air pollution regulations — a consideration that is especially important when an agency has very little coercive authority and must rely largely on voluntary compliance to achieve its regulatory goals. In its inception, at least, cooperation with the groups it is trying to control may thus be functional for a regulatory agency. It becomes dysfunctional only when, at some further point in the relationship, an agency modifies or even abandons its goals in order to retain group support.

Generally speaking, in the case of clientele, regulatory, and other administrative agencies, the tendency for capture by an outside group to take place is greatest when an agency deals with a single-interest constituency. In a case of this kind, an agency has nowhere else to turn if the group upon which it depends should threaten to withdraw its support. Diversification of support is as desirable for a government agency as product diversification is for a private business firm that is anxious to minimize the impact that shifts in consumer taste will have if it sells only a single product. Consider the case of grazing administration:

> . . . The Grazing Service suffered because of its rather complete dependence on stockmen and those who spoke for them in Congress. By merging the Service into an expanded Bureau of Land Management, an act accomplished with the aid of interests adversely affected under the previous arrangement, the new organization has reduced its dependence by being able to appeal to a broader constituency.[18]

The heterogeneity of an administrative agency's group support thus seems to be more important in determining its freedom of action than the question of whether it is organized on the basis of clientele, purpose, process, or area to be served. The design of its political system, rather than its organizational structure, is the critical consideration.

For all agencies it is highly important to keep abreast of changes in the structure of interests affected by the activities they carry on. Huntington traces the administrative decline of the Interstate Commerce Commission to the failure of the agency to develop support among the new transportation interests that emerged in the twentieth century as a result of technological change — the truckers, the water carriers, and the airlines. Instead, the agency tied itself to the railroads — a declining industry it had been originally created to curb in the nineteenth century but that it now spent more and more of its time trying to resuscitate. "The ICC," Huntington says, "has not responded to the demands of the new forces in transportation. . . . Consequently, it is losing its leadership to those agencies that are more responsive to the needs and demands of the times."[19] The establishment of the Department of Transportation in the 1960s as the major transportation agency of the national government provided striking confirmation of this argument.

Public Interest Groups. The relationships described here between executive agencies and their constituencies have long presented American democracy with some of its most perplexing problems. At its best this interaction enhances the representative character of government. Agencies serve as advocates for major community groups and in this way insure that the interests of these groups are not neglected when governmental decisions are being made. While legislators represent citizens grouped together in particular geographic localities, administrative agencies usually represent them in terms of their productive role in society — in a variety of professions and occupations and in innumerable subcategories of activity in the broad fields of business, agriculture, and labor.

Viewed in this way, the executive branch provides a system of representation based on economic and social role, supplementing the territorial representation furnished by Congress and other legislative bodies.[20] This system might be criticized as being redundant on the grounds that the executive is performing a task that the legislature already carries on. But it is doing so in a different way —

representing people in terms of what they do rather than where they live. At the least, this is a useful sort of redundancy, since it sensitizes and more finely tunes the governmental apparatus to the intensity and variety of citizen concerns and needs.[21] Matthew Holden argues that it is in the interest of agencies to seek out groups that are not presently part of any executive constituency, since the attachment of these groups to an agency's following will add to its strength and security.[22] In this way the selfish interest of agencies in expanding the size of their constituency coincides with the pursuit of a more representative government.

But there is a dark side also to the close intimacy between agencies and their publics, and it has been starkly drawn.[23] At its worst — in the case of the captive agency phenomenon already discussed — the relationship degenerates into the transfer of public authority to private groups that use it to advance their own interests at the expense of the general public. When this occurs, an executive agency becomes simply the governmental outpost of an enclave of private power — only able to exercise its public authority at the sufferance of private groups. As a result there may be a total neglect of the public interest in administrative decision-making, and an underrepresentation of groups in society that are too weak to compel an executive agency to heed their complaints.

One of the most important developments that has taken place in American politics in this connection has been the rise to power in recent years of public interest organizations — groups like Common Cause and the cluster of reform organizations sponsored if not actually managed by Ralph Nader. While much of the activity of these groups has been directed at the legislature, they have also played an extremely important role in monitoring the activities of executive agencies. Spokesmen for public interest groups have criticized the preferential treatment agencies often give to powerful private groups, and pressured them to expand their conception of their clientele to include the public-at-large and disadvantaged groups whose needs have not previously figured large in administrative decision-making.

The influence public interest groups have been able to exercise upon executive agencies stems in no small measure from their ability to arouse the indignation and rally the support of their followers through the media of mass communication. The news media

have been a tremendously important factor in the ascending power
of public interest organizations. They provide an avenue through
which an alleged misuse of administrative power can be quickly
and widely publicized. Moreover, investigative reporters often work
together with public interest organizations to expose misconduct in
office, whether it be by an agency like the FTC, which is felt to be
insufficiently vigilant in enforcing consumer protection legislation,[24]
or a water resource agency like the Corps of Engineers, which has
been charged by conservationists with neglecting environmental interests in constructing dams, dredging ˙harbors, and other activities.[25]

One point that needs to be borne in mind in assessing these
efforts to push executive agencies toward responsiveness to a
broader public is that the administration of a good many governmental functions demands a certain narrowness in perspective on
the part of an executive agency. For example, a public agency
charged with responsibility for administering a program of assistance for the handicapped will be expected to give priority and
preference to the needs of its special clientele. Such specialization in
viewpoint would not ordinarily be regarded as inconsistent with
the pursuit of the public interest. Moreover, it is widely accepted
that competition within the executive branch from a variety of
agencies advocating support for special groups is a necessary part
of the entire process through which the public interest can ultimately be determined.

Perhaps the most important single function that public interest
groups perform is to provide the reform impulse with an ongoing
presence in the governmental process. In a celebrated analysis of
what he terms political "quiescence," Murray Edelman argues that
reformers have traditionally tended to be satisfied with merely
symbolic rewards for their political efforts.[26] For example, they tend
to lose interest in politics once they have succeeded in establishing
a regulatory agency, because this achievement gives them a false
sense of reassurance that the public is now being protected against
exploitation. A typical result of this dissipation of reform energy
is that the agency's decisions become more and more sympathetic to
the regulated groups with which it is dealing on a continuing basis.
However, with the rise of public interest groups, the reform spirit
may be said to have become permanently institutionalized. Under
the watchful eye of these groups, the day-to-day decisions of regu-

latory agencies can be made to correspond much more closely with the public interest, and reformers may begin to obtain more than a merely symbolic return on their investment in political activity.

LEGISLATIVE SUPPORT

The legislature is a source of political strength for administration in essentially two ways. In the first place, it is from laws enacted by the legislature that agencies derive their basic legal powers — to give advice to policy-makers, to exercise regulatory authority, or to provide services to the public. Such laws often determine as well the organizational structure of an agency and its ability to hire personnel, or to engage in a host of other housekeeping activities. Law is a fundamental basis of administrative authority, and it is the legislature that, initially at least, writes the law.

A second reason for administrative dependence upon legislative support is the fact that the money which administrative agencies need to fuel their activities must come through the avenue of appropriation bills passed by the legislature. No matter how broad the scope of an agency's formal authority, its real power turns ultimately upon its fiscal resources. A regulatory agency left without adequate funds to enforce the law that it administers has the shadow but not the substance of power. Similarly, the range of services any agency can provide is determined ultimately by the money it is authorized to spend. Money talks, in administration as elsewhere.

The power of Congress in this respect was greatly strengthened when the Supreme Court held in 1975 that the president had no power to impound funds that were clearly authorized for expenditure by Congress. This case, as well as many others, grew out of the Nixon administration's strategy of refusing to expend funds for agencies and programs it disliked, or felt were funded at too high a level, even though appropriations had been voted by Congress. If the court had upheld the broad view of impoundment taken by the Nixon regime, the importance of congressional appropriations for executive agencies would have been greatly reduced. The White House would then have had discretion to determine whether or not an agency would actually get the money Congress had voted, and executive organizations would have to look primarily to it rather than to Congress for financial support.

As indicated in the previous section, high standing with the public gives any agency substantial leverage in dealing with the legislature. However, legislative support is not simply a function of public favor. As the work of Richard Fenno on the appropriation process in Congress clearly reveals, an agency can have a great deal of outside support without enjoying a corresponding esteem with influential elites in the legislature. Conversely, there are a number of agencies that are held in very high regard in Congress but leave the public largely indifferent.[27]

Fenno used two yardsticks for measuring agency success in dealing with the House Appropriations Committee and ultimately with Congress itself. The first was the percentage of its request for appropriations that an administrative agency was successful in obtaining from the House Committee. A number of agencies that scored very high in this regard are very little known in the outside community. The Bureau of Customs is one example in this category, and the Bureau of the Public Debt is another. Both of these agencies are in the Treasury Department, which has intimate ties with Congress while not having a great deal of visibility with the public generally.

A second index used by Fenno for measuring administrative success in the legislature was the rate of growth in the level of financial support that an agency received from the House Appropriations Committee. Here he discovered that there were several agencies with a very high growth rate that nevertheless were subjected to very deep budget cuts annually by the House Committee, so that their appropriations as a percentage of their requests were not as high as those of other agencies with a lower growth rate. Among the agencies included in this category were the Bureau of Land Management, the Fish and Wildlife Service, and the Bureau of Labor Standards. Conversely, a number of the agencies that had been very successful in avoiding budget cuts showed very little increase in their appropriations over the years.

Success in avoiding cuts from appropriations requests is not, therefore, the same as the ability to obtain a continuously expanding level of support from the House Committee responsible for appropriations. The difference between these two criteria of success is explained by Fenno in these terms: *"High growth rates can be accounted for primarily by factors external to the Committee, whereas the ability to keep budget cuts to a minimum can be accounted for primarily by factors internal to the Committee-agency relationship."* [28] An agency's success in fending off budget cuts in the House is a measure of its good rapport with legislators. Its ability to maintain a continuing increase in its appropriations reflects an expanding demand for its services by significant segments of the public. Alternatively, high standing in the legislature may coincide with strength in the outside community, so that an agency avoids budget cuts while maintaining a high growth rate in its appropriations; or an agency may have the misfortune of being weak in terms of both legislative and public support, in which event it is subject to both budget cuts and a low appropriations growth rate.

In all of these cases, the legislature reveals itself as 'an independent force of substantial importance in the life of administrative agencies. Good relations with legislators are especially useful when an agency does not enjoy strong support from outside groups, since this rapport provides assurance that an agency's appropriations, while not expanding, will remain reasonably stable. Even agencies with powerful constituencies can help themselves a great deal by cultivating the goodwill of legislators. While congressmen may not be able to prevent the growth of an agency's appropriations as the public demand for its services expands, they can substantially retard this rate of growth by cutting back the agency's budget requests each year.

When an agency does have strong external support, it may use this constituency as a device for bringing pressure to bear upon lawmakers to reverse legislative decisions on appropriations that it considers disadvantageous. Not uncommon, for example, is the practice of cutting back on services provided outside groups in the wake of a legislative cut in appropriations. The reduction in services is designed to provoke protests from the agency's clientele to the legislature, which will bring about a restoration of at least part of the sum cut from the budget, and this tactic often succeeds.

As a variety of studies of the legislative process make clear, the administrative relationship with the legislature is, in the United States at least, largely a relationship with legislative committees, or in some cases even subcommittees.[29] The legislators who must be cultivated are the key men who sit on the committees that have significant power over the agency. The chief aim of administrators here is to win these legislators over to a favorable attitude toward the agency and an appreciation of the skill and dedication with which it carries on its work. In more formal terms, the administrator's goal is to socialize committee members, particularly a committee or subcommittee chairman, to the agency's point of view, so that these legislators may become spokesmen for the organization in Congress.

There is, in fact, no better lobbyist for any administrative agency than a legislator. Thus, the most fortunately situated of all agencies are those that can number legislators in some sense as members of their own organization. Each of the Armed Services, for example, has had the good fortune to have a number of legislators included within its reserve units, and while it is difficult to determine how captive a congressman actually became as a result of his reserve status, this relationship certainly insures an agency of some kind of capital in the form of legislative goodwill. In state administration, a highway department may derive a similar advantage from the fact that some state legislators who are attorneys earn fees from title searches conducted for the department, and other state agencies use devices such as the consultantship to bring legislators within their own organizational network.

The relationship between an administrative agency and legislative committees may vary a great deal from one committee to another. During the Vietnam War military officials testifying before Congress could expect to receive a far more favorable treatment from the Senate Armed Services Committee than they could from the Senate Foreign Relations Committee, a large number of whose members were highly critical of American involvement in Southeast Asia. Relations with any single committee may also change with the passage of time, as the agency or the committee alters its personnel, or as public attitudes toward the agency and its program shift. The arrival of a number of freshmen congressmen on a committee may bring about a much more critical perspective toward the agencies under its jurisdiction.

One of the most consistent differences in the treatment an agency may encounter in Congress is between the committee that considers legislation in the area of its responsibilities and the appropriations subcommittee that decides in effect how much money the agency can spend to achieve its objectives. Usually the legislative committee is program-oriented and is anxious to see that an agency obtains adequate resources with which to achieve its goals, while the appropriations subcommittee is economy-minded and inclined to trim back appropriations that the legislative committee may have authorized. There is great potential for conflict here, and it has flared up on numerous occasions.

An agency may also experience substantial variation in the treatment it receives from the House and Senate. One significant difference between the two branches of the legislature is that the Senate appropriations committee is usually more generous in handling agency requests for financial support than its counterpart unit in the House. Nelson Polsby provides an explanation for this difference: "in the House money bills are seen primarily in the context of assaults on the Treasury; in the Senate, they are seen as financial extensions of programs, as expressions of legitimate social and political demands." [30] One reason why this is so is that members of the House committee specialize in appropriations, while senators also sit on substantive committees and thus deal with programs to which they become attached.

One official who plays an important role for a growing number of executive agencies in their efforts to cultivate legislative support is the congressional liaison officer. The task of this administrative official is essentially that of keeping in touch with legislators, answering their requests for information, providing help to their constituents, or even writing a speech for a congressman. In an increasingly complex bureaucratic apparatus, liaison officials have become almost indispensable in enabling legislators to find their way around the labyrinthine corridors of bureaucracy.[31] It is, however, questionable if liaison officers can relieve departmental executives of any save the routine chores of legislative-executive relations. On matters of critical importance to an agency, such as the passage of legislation affecting the scope of its power, the task of winning legislative support must inevitably be assumed by officials at a high level of responsibility.

Moreover, some departmental executives even complain that liaison officials are a burden as well as a help. Spending, as they do, a great deal of time in congressional offices, liaison personnel may generate a good many requests for assistance that, as one irate executive put it, "might never come to us if our liaison man did not spend a lot of time on Capitol Hill, running into administrative assistants to congressmen." [32]

The preceding analysis of the efforts of administrative agencies to secure legislative support has centered on the essential resources that the legislature controls and agencies seek to obtain — legal authority and appropriations. It should be noted, however, that in its relations with the legislature, an agency is motivated by a desire not only to obtain these positive assets but also to escape certain punitive sanctions that the legislature has the power to inflict. These sanctions include the exposure of the agency to unpleasant publicity through a highly publicized investigation of its shortcomings, the refusal to approve the appointment of agency executives when (as is true of the U.S. Senate) a legislative body possesses this power of confirmation, and the veto of certain financial transactions an agency is contemplating. The dependence of administrative agencies upon legislative goodwill thus springs from negative as well as positive considerations — the desire to escape penalties as well as to obtain rewards.

Of course, in the process of providing executive agencies with appropriations and the other resources they seek, legislators receive in exchange benefits that are of very substantial value to them. No aspect of their role is of greater importance to members of Congress than their relations with their constituency, and there are innumerable ways in which agencies can be of practical assistance in this regard — ranging from help in establishing or retaining a government facility that may represent a major economic asset in a congressman's district to assisting a legislator in answering an inquiry or resolving a vexing problem that one of his or her constituents has with the government.

In the formal theory of American government, the posture of the legislature with respect to the bureaucracy is one of oversight. Congress is supposed to monitor the behavior of bureaucrats to see that they carry out the tasks assigned to them and do not exceed their authority while doing so. For many legislators, however, the oversight role has never been a high priority task, since it does not contribute to their reelection nearly as much as nursing a constituency — being an effective "errand-boy" congressman.[33] Madison's expectation in the *Federalist Papers* was that all government officials would seek always to maximize their own share of power in the political system, but the behavior of modern legislators often seems to belie this assumption.[34] What they often seem to seek is not so much power as safety — tenure in office rather than the vigorous use of the powers of office. Hence, the attitude of many congressmen toward the executive agencies under their jurisdiction is that they are assets they must protect rather than organizations they must oversee.

But however lightly some congressmen may regard their role as overseers, executive agencies themselves tend to look toward the Hill with considerable anxiety — as a place where one can find powerful friends, or encounter dangerous enemies. An invitation to testify before Congress is an event for which careful preparation is made. A call from a congressman's office requesting information is given very special attention and treatment. Congressional oversight may not look very potent from the perspective of an outsider, but it is taken very seriously in the corridors of bureaucracy.

POWER IN THE EXECUTIVE BRANCH

Through the assiduous cultivation of legislative and public support, it is possible for an administrative agency to establish a position of virtually complete autonomy within the executive branch. When agencies like the FBI and the Corps of Engineers succeeded in doing this, they became largely immune from the hierarchical controls exercised by either the president or officials in their own executive department. Historically, therefore, the quest for outside support has often been a divisive force within the organizational structure of American national bureaucracy, weakening the identification of departments with the president or of bureaus with their department. Agencies that use outside support to acquire a position of independence within the executive branch may ultimately come to regard themselves as being in some sense congressional rather than presidential agencies.

There are of course administrative units at the other extreme that possess virtually no independent standing with the public or the legislature. Performing functions that are primarily useful within the executive branch itself, they remain almost entirely presidential in their orientation. The purest cases of this type are the staff agencies of the presidency, for example, the Council of Economic Advisers. If the president does not choose to give a staff unit like this any power, then it has little or no influence. Of these agencies it can truly be said that the president is their only constituent, and their power can, therefore, fluctuate a great deal between one chief executive and another.

Most agencies, however, do not fall squarely into either of these categorical extremes. They have not formed such strong alliances with outside groups as to become entirely independent of presidential control, nor are they wholly dependent upon their standing as executive agencies for their vitality. Occupying a middle position, they seek to draw strength from sources inside as well as outside the executive branch. While not doing anything to jeopardize their ties with the legislature, they nevertheless seek to maintain strong lines of support with the White House.

One of the best measures of an agency's strength in dealing with the president is the extent to which the White House has to bargain with it in order to secure its cooperation. During the withdrawal of American troops from Vietnam, President Nixon was obliged to make many concessions to the armed services in order to maintain their support for his troop withdrawal program. Moreover, in order to secure Department of Defense acceptance of disarmament agreements that were being negotiated with the Soviet Union, the White House had to give strong support to the department's demand for the continued development of strategic weapons. Indeed, the secretary of defense insisted in testimony before Congress that the department would oppose an arms control agreement if the increased appropriations necessary to continue a weapons development program were not forthcoming. The administration was thus put in the paradoxical position of supplementing the presentation of a disarmament treaty to Congress with a proposal for increased military appropriations.

Agencies also seek support from housekeeping units that have partial control over resources upon which they depend for their operational effectiveness. The Office of Management and Budget (OMB), for example, exercises powers that are of vital importance to every other executive agency. The annual hearings it conducts in the process of framing the executive budget provide a basis for determining how much money each agency needs during the ensuing fiscal year, and this determination by OMB usually becomes a ceiling on the appropriations that an agency can expect to receive from Congress. As noted earlier, all agencies must clear their communications with the legislature through OMB so that the consistency of these communications with the president's policy goals can be checked. The budget agency also has the power to recommend to the president whether he should veto legislation enacted by Congress — legislation that will inevitably affect the fortunes of executive agencies. Finally, OMB conducts studies of the efficiency of executive operations that may well lead to reorganization proposals that will greatly alter the power and status of the agencies affected.[35]

Hence, good relations with the Office of Management and Budget are an invaluable asset for any executive agency. Other staff units that also control resources of value to executive agencies include the Civil Service Commission, which administers personnel regulations that affect an agency's ability to recruit and retain employees, and the General Services Administration, which constructs and operates most government buildings. Of course, in dealing with all these housekeeping units an agency may not be without bargaining power of its own. Aaron Wildavsky's study of the budgetary process shows, for example, that the Bureau of the Budget (now OMB) tended to be generous with those agencies with which it felt Congress would itself be generous. As Wildavsky put it: "The Bureau finds itself treating agencies it dislikes much better than those it may like better but who cannot help themselves nearly as much in Congress." [36] An agency's high standing in the legislature may thus be reflected in the treatment it receives at the hands of a staff agency that is presumably responsive to the interests of the president alone — a striking illustration of the extent of legislative influence upon executive behavior and decisions.

As far as individual bureaus are concerned, relations with the hierarchy of the department in which they are located is also of strategic importance. While the phenomenon of "bureau autonomy" has not vanished from American bureaucracy, there has certainly been a secular trend toward increasing the power and capacity of departmental officials to control the activities of bureaus under their jurisdiction. Through successive reorganization measures, bureaus have been clustered together in more homogeneous department groupings where they can be subject to more effective supervision; the size and authority of departmental staffs have been strengthened; and legal powers that once resided in the bureaus have been moved upward into the hands of the department.

Moreover, since World War II there has been a steady growth in a new science of management in the public service. Its methods include operations research, systems analysis, the extensive use of program budgeting and cost analysis as a prerequisite to making expenditure decisions, the employment of computers wherever possible in the management process, and the establishment of research units to gather information systematically as a basis for evaluating the performance of subordinate units. These management techniques have greatly enhanced the capacity of departments for overhead control, and have generally had a centralizing effect upon the operations of American bureaucracy.

But these changes have not affected the power of all bureaus to the same degree, and they have certainly not been uniform with respect to all departments. Moreover, there are some current trends that are highly decentralizing in their impact. The growth in professionalism in government employment has tended to make many bureaus more specialized, and hence more difficult for generalists in the department hierarchy to control. The activities of natural scientists working at the bureau level are not easily monitored by lay administrators in departmental headquarters units. Witness, for example, a department like Health, Education, and Welfare, where the high degree of professionalism at the bureau level — in medicine, science, welfare, and educational specialties — has long tended to frustrate efforts to establish departmental authority.

The structure of power within the executive branch can thus be looked at from the perspective of the vertical distribution of authority — with attention focused upon either the ability of a president and his staff agencies to influence the decisions and behavior of bureaucrats at lower echelons, or the extent of control that department officials can exert over their own bureaus. Looked at in this way, the executive branch presents a picture today of bureaus possessing a great deal of independent authority, based among other things on the fact that bureau chiefs generally have much longer tenure in office than do departmental officials, but with a constantly expanding overlay of centralized controls.

It is also possible to look at power in the executive branch in terms of the lateral distribution of influence — between agencies located at approximately the same hierarchical rank but with responsibility for different programs. From this perspective, there are certain possibilities for conflict or cooperation between administrative units, and an agency's success in turning these situations to its advantage will go far to determine its real power or status within the executive branch.

Lateral conflicts between administrative units often arise because these agencies are pursuing goals that are diametrically opposed. The Anti-Trust Division of the Department of Justice, for example, has been in frequent conflict with one or another of the regulatory agencies that administer statutes covering a single major industry within the economy. The division has opposed the merger of business firms when this would seem to have a negative effect on economic competition, while agencies like the Interstate Commerce Commission or the Federal Power Commission have been quite sympathetic to such mergers when they have appeared to promise the emergence of a stronger and more stable industry. Here administrative conflict is a function of a long-standing ambivalence in public policy, because some executive agencies have been charged with promoting economic competition, while others have been allowed to protect selected industries from the hazards and uncertainties of the competitive life.

Interagency conflicts are also likely to arise when two agencies pursue goals that are not opposing but closely related. Here conflict occurs for the same reason that it prevails in the private economy — agencies are competitors. This competition may take place in a variety of areas — over questions of jurisdiction, for the support of outside groups, or in the quest for presidential or congressional favor. Competition of this sort has given rise to some of the most celebrated interagency conflicts in American administrative history. The ancient struggle between the Corps of Engineers and the Bureau of Reclamation is perhaps the classic case of this kind, as these two agencies fought for jurisdiction over water resource projects.[37] Similar conflicts have broken out between the Forest Service and the Bureau of Land Management over administration of public lands in the West,[38] and between the Extension Division and the Soil Conservation Service in the Department of Agriculture over agricultural policy.[39]

In some areas of policy, agencies administering closely related functions develop a "separate spheres of interest" doctrine as a means of avoiding jurisdictional conflict. Two state universities, for example, may emphasize different educational programs as their chief responsibility, as has traditionally been the case in Indiana, or, as in California, the university and state college systems may be set up to serve students with different records of academic achievement. Of course, the equilibrium produced by this arrangement does not always remain stable. In modern times, state agricultural colleges have almost universally aspired to be full-fledged universities, and this has frequently triggered conflict with the existing state university. "Have-not" organizations, like "have-not" nations, are particularly likely to violate any spheres of interest agreement when an opportunity presents itself to improve their position vis-à-vis a stronger competitor.

One point that should be noted is that some agencies may have other agencies as part of their clientele. For example, national agencies that dispense grants to state or local units have these organizations as perhaps their most important constituents. Charles Jones has pointed this out with respect to state and local air pollution agencies: "Part of an emerging national network of control, they receive funds, technical aid, training, and support from the federal agency. Further, they are potential sources of support as well as potential organizers of support among the public." [40] The same situation prevails with respect to other national agencies administering grants-in-aid programs. When state agencies receiving such grants are joined together in an interstate organization, they constitute a formidable lobby in Washington, capable of exercising great influence over policy development at the national level.

The relations between executive agencies need not necessarily be competitive. Since many agencies have common or complementary interests that bind them together, they may establish an informal alliance for the achievement of their objectives. Sometimes agencies, like nations, may negotiate such alliances even though there is a long history of hostility between them. As in international relations, this occurs most frequently when a common danger arises that threatens both of them more than each endangers the other.

For example, in 1944 those life-long antagonists, the Corps of Engineers and the Bureau of Reclamation, were able to arrive at a mutually agreeable arrangement for the development of water resources in the Missouri Valley area. The treaty they signed for this purpose was called the Pick-Sloan plan, and it was forced upon them by, among other considerations, the threat that an agency like the Tennessee Valley Authority might soon be established to take over all water resource activities in the Missouri River area. Labeled by one of its critics as "a shameless, loveless shotgun wedding," this treaty between the bureau and the corps helped to dissipate whatever real possibility existed that a valley authority might be given comprehensive jurisdiction over water resource administration in the Missouri basin.[41] Bilateral and multilateral alliances of this sort may often be as essential to an organization's survival as they are to the defense of a nation's security.

Cooperation between executive agencies may also be initiated more formally by legislative or executive action requiring two or more agencies to work together to handle a single program. In state government, for example, some programs are still carried on through administrative boards or commissions on which several departments are represented. In metropolitan areas, public organizations in individual localities commonly belong to areawide councils through which a great deal of interorganizational cooperation can take place. At the national level, a variety of interdepartmental committees have been established to handle problems that require joint consideration by several agencies for their solution.

In cases of this sort where agencies are brought together as a result of legislative or executive order, the interdepartmental committee in which they are included may become a theater of conflict rather than an instrument of cooperation. In describing national security affairs, where the State, Defense, Treasury, and other executive departments have been yoked together on many interdepartmental committees by the president or Congress, the Senate Subcommittee on National Policy Machinery wrote:

> Inter-agency committees are the gray and bloodless ground of bureaucratic warfare — a warfare of position, not of decisive battles. State commonly sees them as devices for bringing "outsiders" into matters it regards as its own, and resists encroachment. The other departments and agencies use them as instruments for "getting into the act." [42]

Formal interdepartmental cooperation that is enforced upon executive agencies may thus serve to mask bitter and protracted warfare between them.

But these cases of conflict should not obscure the fact that in a variety of bureaucratic settings agencies have found it possible to establish very cooperative relations based on systems of exchange. Very commonly what agencies exchange is a single commodity that is useful to both of them, such as information. Law enforcement agencies need to trade a great deal of data in order to carry out the task of apprehending criminals, and public health officials may find it similarly useful in planning for the best use of hospitals in a metropolitan area.[43]

Sometimes the commodities that agencies exchange are quite dissimilar in character. A study of interorganizational exchanges in which the State Department was involved showed a number of such transactions, including an agreement under which the department assisted the National Aeronautics and Space Administration in locating suitable sites for space tracking stations around the world, in return for NASA lending the department the services of its astronauts for goodwill missions abroad.[44]

Of course, there are areas of administration where exchange is very difficult. In the intelligence community, for example, an agency may regard the information it possesses as the core of its power and be unwilling to share this data with what it regards as rival organizations. The CIA justified its excursion into domestic intelligence — an activity barred to it by the statute under which it was established — on the grounds that the FBI would not pass on information in its files on alleged subversive activity in the United States. The establishment of such "information screens" to conceal data is common when agencies regard information as not only an element of power but as synonymous with it. They are much less reluctant to trade a commodity like information when they perceive it as having little value for them.

EXPERTISE, POLITICS, AND POWER

In the preceding chapters a distinction has been drawn between the influence administrative agencies exercise as a result of their professional skills and the power they acquire through the development of political support. These two sources of bureaucratic power, expertise, and politics, while easy to distinguish in analysis, are not as readily separated in the actual practice of executive agencies. More often than not, they are so linked together as sources of influence that it is difficult to tell how much of an agency's impact upon policy stems from its expertise and how much rests on the size and strength of its political constituency.

Military officers, for example, are what Morris Janowitz calls "professionals in violence." [45] They have a great deal of influence over the framing of national security policy purely because of their mastery of the art and science of warfare, and of the use of force to accomplish national objectives. Hence, their role in the policy process would be strategic whether or not they had any constituency at all. But in modern American society at least, the power of the professional soldier has been enormously enhanced by the formidable network of outside support each of the military services has managed to cultivate. This network includes congressmen and congressional committees with responsibilities in national security matters, industrial firms that are dependent upon defense contracts, and the so-called "back-stop associations" of the military — the Navy League and the Army and Air Force Associations. These and other groups collectively represent the "military-industrial" complex that has received so much attention in contemporary American politics.

The power of this military industrial complex can easily be exaggerated, since on many issues of national security policy the military point of view has not prevailed, and with regard to specific issues the military often generates a variety of policy perspectives. But certainly military officers do have substantial influence over the framing of national security policy. What is perhaps impossible to know is how much of this influence simply reflects the pressures of the military lobby behind the Pentagon and how much springs from deference accorded military expertise itself.

Whatever the relative weight of expertise and politics as sources of bureaucratic power, all executive agencies in the United States recognize the value of political support, and devote a great deal of energy to seeking out and nursing a constituency. The extent to which American bureaucracy is thus politicized reflects the fact that a democratic political system was already well established in this country when a bureaucracy of substantial size first began to emerge in the latter part of the nineteenth century. The development of political skills was part of the process by which executive agencies adapted to their environment in order to survive in the egalitarian democratic society in which they found themselves.

This American experience stands in stark contrast to the historical development of bureaucracy in European democratic states. There a highly developed bureaucratic apparatus commonly existed and played a large role in governing the state long before the advent of democratic political institutions. In Europe it was democracy that had to accommodate itself to the presence of a strongly entrenched bureaucratic system. Partly because they enjoyed a security of position that American bureaucracies lacked, and partly because of the conventions of the parliamentary system, executive agencies in European states have historically had less reason and

less opportunity to engage in direct political activity of the sort
that is so common in the United States.

But if a politicized bureaucracy is deeply rooted in the American
political tradition, so too is a considerable degree of deference to
expertise in the governing process. The creation of a variety of
political institutions in the United States — including the council-
manager form of government in urban communities, the special-
authority device in both state and local government, and the independent regulatory commissions at the national level — testifies to
the fact that it is very much in the American grain to attempt to
defuse political controversy by transforming political issues into
technical problems. Both city and county managers are expected to
furnish their local area with professional government based on nonpolitical criteria, and the special authority and the independent
regulatory commissions have both been set up to take government
away from the politicians and put it in the hands of the experts.
The appointment by presidents of special commissions to study and
report on major issues of public policy also reflects this national
faith in expertise.

Since World War II at least, expertise has certainly played a
dominant role in foreign or national security policy, where the involvement of domestic political groups often takes place only after
a decision has been made. Most decisions are reached in secret, and
public opinion is acquainted with what has transpired only through
"leaks" — which may come from executive officials who disapprove
of what has been decided and are trying to reverse the decision by
arousing public opinion against it.

Bureaucratic experts of various kinds thus exercise a pervasive
influence over national security decisions. These professional groups
include diplomats, military officers, scientists, and what Bernard
Brodie calls "scientific strategists." [46] As Samuel P. Huntington de-
scribes the development of national defense strategy: "The relative
absence of nongovernmental groups concerned with strategy enhances the extent and the importance of the bargaining roles of
governmental officials and agencies." [47] In this case public participation in actual policy decisions tends to be indirect. The public par-
ticipates as the officials making decisions take potential public reactions into account in reaching their own conclusions. While the
public is not likely to question the competence of government
officials to define the national interest, it is quite capable of

eventual resentment against the sacrifices and burdens any international involvement may entail.

In many areas of domestic policy-making, on the other hand, a variety of nongovernmental groups take a continuous interest in the policy-making processes of administrative agencies. As noted earlier, this relationship is in many instances initiated by the agencies themselves. The views of an agency's public can thus be incorporated into the initial design of policy. In fact bureaucratic policy-making in such areas commonly represents a reconciliation of conflicting group interests as much as it does the application of expertise toward the solution of particular problems.

This distinction between policy-making in the administration of foreign and domestic affairs should not be exaggerated. Bureaucrats in the national security area enjoy somewhat more freedom from outside political pressures in at least the early stages of their deliberations. But these pressures are never entirely absent from any area of bureaucratic decisions in the United States, so wide and well-traveled are the channels of access between administrative agencies on the one hand and the community on the other.

It seems clear that there are important variations in the relative weight of expertise and political activity as sources of bureaucratic power at different levels of government in the American federal system. By and large, administrative agencies in the states and localities are much more intimately involved in the political process than are similar units at the national level. It is still common in state and local government for the heads of administrative agencies to be elected rather than appointed, and this practice inevitably politicizes the atmosphere in which administration is carried on. Moreover, in some of the more backward jurisdictions, patronage is still rife, and agencies serve mainly as auxiliaries for the party organizations. The employees of administrative agencies represent, in any case, a sizable group in state and local politics, and the votes of employee organizations of policemen, firemen, or teachers can easily play a decisive role in local elections.

It is also standard practice for issues as well as offices to be voted upon in state and local elections, and many of these issues are of salient importance to one or more administrative agencies. A school system will lend every effort to secure the passage of a school bond issue on a local ballot, and all agencies face at every election the possibility of becoming involved in a struggle over a public expenditure issue, a referendum, or a constitutional amendment affecting their power or the scope of their activity. However politicized national agencies may be in other ways, they are nevertheless insulated from such election contests. The FBI, for example, while adept at many aspects of political activity, does not, like a local police department, have to concern itself with the success or failure of items on the ballot that critically affect the status of the organization and its members.

There are marked differences in the sources of bureaucratic power not only between national administration and agencies at lower echelons of government but also among agencies at the state and local level. For example, there are many rural states where administrative agencies are highly politicized and where little tendency yet exists to develop or defer to bureaucratic expertise. In urban, industrialized states, on the other hand, the professionalization of bureaucracy is often quite advanced, and the operations of administrative agencies have been sealed off from the cruder kinds of political pressure.[48]

Similar variations exist with respect to local government. From their study of New York City, Wallace S. Sayre and Herbert Kaufman conclude that the city's bureaucracies play a key role in its political life.

> Extending the merit system of employment for city employees has had . . . a history of steady and eventually almost complete acceptance in the city's government. . . . The consequences have included not merely the anticipated increase in competence and conventional rationality in the conduct of the city government, but also, and equally significant, the rise of a new form of political power in the city: the career bureaucracies, and especially the organized bureaucracies. Once closely allied to, and greatly dependent upon, the party leaders, the bureaucracies now have the status and the capacity of autonomous participants in the city's political process.[49]

Studies of other cities do not show bureaucracies exerting a comparable degree of influence in the policy process. From Robert A. Dahl's study of New Haven, it is almost impossible to tell if the city has a bureaucracy, so invisible is it in his account of the governing process of the community.[50] Both Edward C. Banfield's analysis of Chicago and M. Kent Jennings' examination of Atlanta assign a more important role to the bureaucratic component in the policy process, but it is still far less significant than that which Sayre and Kaufman depict in New York.[51]

Assuming that these findings are in all cases correct, the strong position of the bureaucracy in the government of New York may be traced to the extraordinary size of the city, and the necessity this imposes for the devolution of authority to administrative agencies. Or the critical factor may be the sharp cleavage between reform and Tammany machine politics in New York's governmental tradition, which led, first, to the practice of giving public agencies strong guarantees in law and custom against political interference, and, second, to the conversion by the bureaucracies of this protection into a mandate for virtually complete autonomy for themselves in the governing process.

In any case, cities differ across the country in the scope of the power that administrative agencies enjoy and in the sources of this power. Parallel differences exist among the states, and between state and national administration. It seems safe to say that bureaucratic expertise varies directly in the United States with the size of the population and the complexity of the environment being governed. The national bureaucracy is more technically proficient than are, on the whole, state administrative agencies, while the states at the same time are more expert at administration than their own rural units of local government. Cities on the other hand are more likely to have highly skilled bureaucracies than rural states — given the environmental complexity and population expansion that urbanization both reflects and engenders. Hence, as governmental jurisdictions become more urbanized, the need for bureaucratic expertise grows apace, and there is an increasing tendency for the power of administrative agencies to rest upon deference to their expertise as well as upon the cultivation of political support.

Notes

1. Norton Long, *The Polity* (Chicago: Rand McNally & Co., 1962), p. 53. The best study of the origins, structure, and operation of the outside groups with which executive agencies deal is James Q. Wilson, *Political Organizations* (New York: Basic Books, 1973).

2. For a careful analysis of this development over the course of American history, see Herbert Kaufman, "The Growth of the Federal Personnel System," in Wallace Sayre, ed., *The Federal Government Service* (Englewood Cliffs, N.J.: Prentice-Hall, 1965), pp. 7–69.

3. For analysis of the power of government publicity, see Francis E. Rourke, *Secrecy and Publicity: Dilemmas of Democracy* (Baltimore: The Johns Hopkins Press, 1961); Delmer D. Dunn, *Public Officials and the Press* (Reading Mass.: Addison-Wesley, 1969); Leon V. Sigal, *Reporters and Officials: The Organization and Politics of Newsmaking* (Lexington, Mass.: Lexington Books, D. C. Heath and Co., 1973).

4. Anthony Downs, "Up and Down with Ecology — the 'Issue Attention Cycle,'" *The Public Interest* 28 (Summer 1972): 38–50.

5. E. E. Schattschneider, *The Semisoverign People* (New York: Holt, Rinehart and Winston, 1960).

6. Charles O. Jones, "The Limits of Public Support: Air Pollution Agency Development," *Public Administration Review* XXXII (September/October 1972): 502–8.

7. See Phillip O. Foss, *Politics and Grass* (Seattle: University of Washington Press, 1960).

8. See W. O. Chittick, *State Department, Press, and Pressure Groups* (New York: John Wiley & Sons, 1970), esp. chap. 8.

9. See Richard E. Neustadt, *Presidential Power* (New York: John Wiley & Sons, 1960), pp. 49–50.

10. See David B. Truman, *The Governmental Process* (New York: Alfred A. Knopf, 1951), pp. 90–92.

11. Francis E. Rourke, "The Department of Labor and the Trade Unions," *The Western Political Quarterly* VII (December 1954): 661–62.

12. Samuel P. Huntington, *The Common Defense: Strategic Programs in National Politics* (New York: Columbia University Press, 1961), p. 397.

13. Ibid., p. 400.

14. For an analysis of the role of leaks in the relationship between executive agencies and the media see Sigal, *Reporters and Officials*, pp. 143–48, and Morton B. Halperin, *Bureaucratic Politics and Foreign Policy* (Washington, D.C.: The Brookings Institution, 1974), pp. 173–95.

15. Philip Selznick, *TVA and the Grass Roots* (Berkeley: University of California Press, 1949).

16. Philip Selznick, *Leadership in Administration* (Evanston, Ill.: Row, Peterson & Co., 1957), p. 44.

17. For an analysis of this tendency in regulatory agencies, see Marver H. Bernstein, *Regulating Business by Independent Commission* (Princeton, N.J.: Princeton University Press, 1955), pp. 74–102. Bernstein argues that all regulatory agencies go through a "life cycle" in which capture by the regulated groups is a culminating phase.

18. Aaron Wildavsky, *The Politics of the Budgetary Process* (Boston: Little, Brown and Co., 1974), p. 172.

19. Samuel P. Huntington, "The Marasmus of the I.C.C.: The Commission, the Railroads, and the Public Interest," *Yale Law Journal* 61 (April 1952): 472–73.

20. For an interesting discussion of the executive role in representation see Roger H. Davidson, "Congress and the Executive: The Race for Representation," in Alfred DeGrazia, coord., *Twelve Studies of the Organization of Congress* (Washington, D.C.: The American Enterprise Institute for Public Policy Research, 1966).

21. For a compelling argument in behalf of redundancy in the design and operation of governmental institutions, see Martin Landau, "Redundancy, Rationality, and the Problem of Duplication and Overlap," *Public Administration Review* 29 (July/August 1969): 346–58.

22. Matthew Holden, "Imperialism in Bureaucracy," *American Political Science Review* 60 (December 1966): 943–51.

23. The disadvantageous aspects of this relationship are clearly spelled out in Grant McConnell, *Private Power and American Democracy* (New York: Alfred A. Knopf, 1966), and Theodore J. Lowi, *The End of Liberalism* (New York: W. W. Norton and Co., 1969).

24. Edward Cox, Robert Fellmeth, and John Schulz, *The Nader Report on the Federal Trade Commission* (New York: Grove Press, 1970). There are a great many task force reports by Nader study groups on other executive agencies, including the National Institute of Mental Health, the U.S. Forest Service, and the Interstate Commerce Commission.

25. See Walter A. Rosenbaum, *The Politics of Environmental Concern* (New York: Praeger Publishers, 1973), esp. pp. 172–89.

26. Murray Edelman, *The Symbolic Uses of Politics* (Urbana, Ill.: The University of Illinois Press, 1964).

27. Richard F. Fenno, *The Power of the Purse* (Boston: Little, Brown and Co., 1966). For additional information see also a more recent book by Fenno, *Congressmen in Committees* (Boston: Little, Brown and Co., 1973).

28. Fenno, *The Power of the Purse*, p. 404.

29. Ibid., p. xvi. "No generalizations about Congress are voiced more frequently or held more firmly than those which proclaim the dominance of committee influence in congressional decision-making."

30. Nelson W. Polsby, *Congress and the Presidency* (Englewood Cliffs, N.J.: Prentice-Hall, 1971), p. 126.

31. G. Russell Pipe, "Congressional Liaison: The Executive Branch Consolidates Its Relations with Congress," *Public Administration Review* XXVI (March 1966): 17, and Abraham H. Holtzman, *Legislative Liaison* (Chicago: Rand McNally & Co., 1970).

32. Marver H. Bernstein, *The Job of the Federal Executive* (Washington, D.C.: The Brookings Institution, 1958), p. 115.

33. For an argument to this effect, see David Mayhew, *Congress: The Electoral Connection* (New Haven: Yale University Press, 1974).

34. See Roy P. Fairfield, ed., *The Federalist Papers* (Garden City, N.Y.: Doubleday Anchor edition, 1961), esp. Federalist No. 51.

35. For a review of the origins and historical development of OMB, see Allen Schick, "The Budget Bureau that Was: Thoughts on the Rise, Decline and Future of a Presidential Agency," in *Papers on the Institutionalized Presidency* (Washington, D.C., The Brookings Institution, 1971), pp. 519–39.

36. Wildavsky, *The Politics of the Budgetary Process*, p. 42.

37. See Arthur Maass, *Muddy Waters* (Cambridge: Harvard University Press, 1951).

38. See Norman Wengert, *Natural Resources and the Political Struggle* (Garden City, N.Y.: Doubleday & Co., 1955), p. 52.

39. See Charles M. Hardin, *The Politics of Agriculture* (Glencoe, Ill.: The Free Press, 1952).

40. Jones, "The Limits of Public Support," p. 503.

41. For an account of the development of the Pick-Sloan plan, see Henry C. Hart, *The Dark Missouri* (Madison: University of Wisconsin Press, 1957), pp. 120–35.

42. U.S. Senate, 87th Cong., 1st sess. *Organizing for National Security.* Study submitted to the Committee on Government Operations United States Senate by its subcommittee on National Policy Machinery, Jan. 28, 1961 (Washington: U.S. Government Printing Office, 1961).

43. See Sol Levine and Paul E. White, "Exchange as a Conceptual Framework for the Study of Interorganizational Relationships," *Administrative Science Quarterly* 5 (March 1961): 583–601.

44. David Davis, *How the Bureaucracy Makes Foreign Policy: An Exchange Analysis* (Lexington, Mass.: Lexington Books, D. C. Heath and Co., 1972).

45. Morris Janowitz, *The Professional Soldier* (New York: Free Press of Glencoe, 1960), pp. 3–16.

46. Bernard Brodie, "The Scientific Strategists," in Robert Gilpin and Christopher Wright eds., *Scientists and National Policy-Making* (New York: Columbia University Press, 1964), pp. 240–56.

47. Samuel P. Huntington, *The Common Defense* (New York: Columbia University Press, 1961), p. 147.

48. For a discussion of these differences between rural and urban states, see Robert B. Highsaw, "The Southern Governor — Challenge to the Strong Executive Theme," *Public Administration Review* 19 (Winter 1959): 7–11. For descriptions of the role of state administrators, see Joseph A. Schlesinger, "The Politics of the Executive," and Ira Sharkansky, "State Administrators in the Political Process," in Herbert Jacob and Kenneth N. Vines, eds., *Politics in the American States* (Boston: Little, Brown and Co., 1971), pp. 210–37, 238–71.

49. Wallace S. Sayre and Herbert Kaufman, *Governing New York City* (New York: Russell Sage Foundation, 1960), p. 732.

50. Robert A. Dahl, *Who Governs?* (New Haven: Yale University Press, 1961).

51. Edward C. Banfield, *Political Influence* (New York: Free Press of Glencoe, 1961, and M. Kent Jennings, *Community Influentials* (New York: Free Press of Glencoe, 1964). For a comprehensive survey of the role of state and local bureaucracies, see Douglas M. Fox, *The Politics of City and State Bureaucracy* (Pacific Palisades, Calif.: Goodyear Publishing Co., 1974).

CHAPTER FOUR

Differentials in Agency Power

While all administrative agencies have at least some of the professional and political assets upon which bureaucratic power depends,
these agencies vary a great deal in their capacity to exercise influence over policy decisions. Some agencies are extraordinarily
gifted in their ability to achieve their goals, while others often seem
to be step-children of the executive branch. At the lowest ebb of its
power, an agency may ultimately come to be "an object of contempt
to its enemies and of despair to its friends." [1]

Several factors help to shape these variations in agency power.
The nature of an agency's expertise is of strategic importance, for
not all bureaucratic skills command equal respect in the community. Moreover, agencies differ a great deal in the nature of their
constituencies. Some organizations simply enjoy the support of
more influential groups than others or have fewer powerful
enemies. Along with these basic resources of expertise and clientele
support, two other factors are highly instrumental in determining
the political effectiveness of an administrative agency. One is an
agency's organizational vitality. Because of the nature of their mission or the dedication of their personnel, some agencies generate a
good deal more energy than others. The second of these instrumental factors is the quality of leadership with which an agency
is blessed. However well-endowed it may be in other respects, an
agency that is not effectively led will fall far short of attaining the
full measure of its potential influence.

While the various factors that help to shape differentials in
agency power can thus be sorted out, there is no easy way in which

the effectiveness of one source of power can be weighed against
another. No common unit of measurement exists for making such
comparisons. This is a problem that arises in connection with all
efforts to measure power or influence.[2] It is not, for example, very
feasible to use the outcomes of disputes between agencies having
apparently different sources of power as a test of the relative value
of one kind of power as opposed to another. In the United States at
least, the abundance of resources makes it possible to have power
contests in which all participants gain at least some of their original
objectives. In any case, a single agency may draw power from
several different sources, and there is no way of telling how much
of an agency's success should be attributed to bureaucratic expertise,
constituency strength, organizational vitality, or skillful leadership.

VARIETIES OF BUREAUCRATIC EXPERTISE

All administrative agencies have some degree of expertise in the
functions they perform, but not all bureaucratic skills exact equal
deference from the community. There are some areas in which the
notion of expertise is lightly regarded. Fields like education and
diplomacy have many self-styled "experts" but very little of what
an outsider would necessarily accept as expertise. Or the amount of
expertise available in the private sector of society may equal or out-
weigh that which a government organization commands. In cases
of this sort, a public agency is not in a strong position to use its
special skills as a source of influence over public policy.

Where there is a lack of respect for the intrinsic function that an
agency performs, the search for clientele support can be particularly
intense since a strong constituency is imperative for a public agency
whose technical proficiency is not held in high esteem. In such a
situation an agency may easily become what Burton Clark has described as a "precarious organization" — constantly obliged to curry
public favor in order to survive.[3] In the California adult education
program that Clark studied, the administrators involved found it
very difficult to adhere to professional standards because of the constant need they faced to satisfy their clientele. Since adult education
lacked legitimacy as part of the regular educational program, survival depended upon an ability to attract a noncaptive student
body. Decisions on curriculum and personnel came to be based on

student demands rather than professional criteria. As Clark explains it: "The adult schools are torn between being a service facility and a school enterprise . . . acceptance is sought on the basis of service rather than on intrinsic educational worth and professional competence." [4]

As a source of power, expertise reaches its fullest development in those organizations that have skills related to the survival of the society. Scientists and military officers, for example, are in a highly advantageous position today to command respect for their particular talents. Professionals in each of these groups exercise powers that may have "life-or-death" consequences for the citizen. In the case of the military professional, the deference that the public accords may be the product of fear as well as respect, since military organizations alone among public agencies have the capacity to take over physical control of the apparatus of the state. They are what Feit has called "armed bureaucrats." [5]

The ascendancy of military professionals within the bureaucracy seems, however, to be a more pronounced characteristic of backward than of advanced societies. In the so-called emerging nations, the military bureaucracy is in a commanding position in the state because it represents the only well-trained elite and is the most efficiently organized institution in the country.[6] In this context, the military bureaucracy is not subject to effective restraint by either a system of political parties or the countervailing power of civilian agencies. The temptation to seize control of the state is strong, and military coups have, therefore, been a prominent feature of the politics of underdeveloped nations.

In a highly industrialized society like the United States, however, with an extremely well-organized and highly literate population, the influence of the military is offset by that of a variety of other groups and organizations. The military is only one of many skilled professions, and its dominance even in the area of national security policy cannot be assured. The standing of any bureaucratic role is thus shaped in part by the stage of political development a society has reached.

It also varies a good deal from one period to another in any particular society. Prior to World War II, American foreign policy was very much the exclusive preserve of the professional diplomat. Following the outbreak of hostilities, however, the military began to exert increasing influence on foreign policy decisions, and since the

war a variety of other skill groups have also come to exercise influence over such decisions. As a result, the Department of State has
been hard put in recent years to maintain its hegemony in the field
of foreign policy. The skills of a diplomat may be much less relevant to the negotiation of a nuclear test ban treaty than those of a
nuclear physicist.

Changes in the state of knowledge play an important part in
bringing about these alterations in the status of a particular skill
group. The emergence of a new managerial science in recent years
— operations research, systems analysis, and a number of other associated techniques — has brought a group of management specialists
to the fore in public as well as in private organizations. During the
Kennedy administration these specialists helped civilian strategists
impose their will on military professionals in decisions involving
arms development. Against such software weaponry as "cost-effectiveness" ratios, traditional military tactics as taught at the service
academies proved virtually helpless. In the Nixon years a similar
group of management experts played a large role in the administration's effort to cut back welfare expenditures.

Two characteristics are especially valuable in enhancing the influence of any body of experts within a bureaucracy. The first is the
possession of a highly technical body of knowledge that the lay-
man cannot readily master, and the second is a capacity to produce
tangible achievements that the average man can easily recognize.
This combination of obscurity in means and clarity of results seems
an irresistible formula for success as far as any professional group is
concerned.

In the period since World War II, the natural scientists have
been the group most strongly exhibiting these two characteristics in
bureaucracy. While these scientists may not be quite the "new
priesthood" some writers have claimed, still there is no doubt about
the prestige and public respect in which the so-called hard sciences
are today held.[7] This standing rests in part upon the awe with
which scientific wizardry is regarded by the general public, and in
part upon the fact that the natural sciences have been — in the
areas of their central concern — so extraordinarily successful in obtaining results, whether in the development of nuclear weapons, the
exploration of space, or the conquest of disease.

Among social scientists, only economists have achieved comparable standing in recent years in the prestige and influence of their

expertise in the framing of public policy.[8] Their role is most highly visible in the work of the Council of Economic Advisers — which is charged with chief responsibility for making recommendations to the president on the larger economic issues of the day, such as the maintenance of a high level of employment. But it is also apparent in the increasing use of economic skills in other areas of administration, such as the cost-benefit analysis and evaluation used in making decisions on the allocation of budgetary resources among administrative agencies. As is the case with natural scientists, the power of economists is a result of the specialized nature of their discipline— and the fact that they have demonstrated a capacity to help elected officials make the hard choices that the development of public policy entails.

ADMINISTRATIVE CONSTITUENCIES

The most obviously important characteristic of any agency's constituency is the effective size of its political following. Differentials in agency power are often alleged to rest more than anything else on the number of people an agency serves as well as upon the strategic dispersion of this clientele around the country. In a comparison of the relative influence of the Corps of Engineers and the Bureau of Reclamation upon water resource policy, Arthur Maass traces the superior influence of the corps precisely to the fact that it provides significant services to a larger and more strategically dispersed clientele.[9] While the irrigation orientation of the bureau has largely confined its activities to the western part of the United States, where rainfall is often sparse, the corps performs not only irrigation but also navigation, flood-control, harbor dredging, and other water resource functions, which give it a substantial following in every section of the country.

The number of congressional districts or states in which an agency's activities are significant often provides a convenient measure of the dimensions of an agency's clientele, where this yardstick can be appropriately used. The power of the Department of Defense in American politics in recent years has often been calculated in precisely this way. Observers have linked the influence of the department with the number of congressional districts in which defense contracts are a significant factor in the local economy. A measure of the department's potential influence in the Senate rather than in the House can be derived by identifying the number of states in which domestic industries are heavily dependent upon defense contracts.

Certainly, the size and dispersion of an agency's clientele have a very significant bearing upon the scope of its influence, and agencies are understandably interested in increasing the geographical spread of their support. The Department of the Interior, for example, has traditionally been regarded in American politics as devoted primarily to the interests of the West. The department's program heavily emphasizes water resource and public land management activities that are chiefly of concern in the western states, and in deference to this geographical identification the secretary of the interior has customarily been selected from the West. However, when the Bureau of Outdoor Recreation was placed under its jurisdiction, the department for the first time gained an administrative foothold in the metropolitan areas in the Northeast where both the population and the demand for outdoor recreation have enormously expanded. The addition of this clientele gave the department an opportunity to serve substantial population groups in a part of the country in which it had not previously played a significant role.

The breadth of an agency's following is not, however, the sole determinant of its ability to provide an agency with political support. To measure the scope of an agency's power, it is necessary to do more than determine how many followers the agency can muster in its own behalf. However large it may be, a clientele that is weak in certain other salient respects will not be in a position to give effective political assistance. A small clientele that is highly self-conscious and dedicated to the pursuit of certain tangible objectives that it shares with the agency can in the last analysis be much more helpful than a large clientele that has neither of these characteristics. For example, consumers as a group represent as large a following as any agency could reasonably hope to command and yet agencies representing consumers have traditionally been weak in their political position, primarily because consumers lacked self-consciousness as a group, were poorly organized, and usually did not have a strong identification with agencies set up to serve their interests.

This situation changed dramatically in recent years as public interest organizations began to make their weight felt in the political system. Consumer advocates like Ralph Nader and public interest lawyers have given the needs of consumers an ongoing representation in Washington to compete with the lobbying efforts of producer groups in Congress and in the corridors of executive agencies. Nader has been involved in the organization of so many groups as to become in effect a public interest conglomerate. Hence, it is no longer as true as it once was that "while all citizens are consumers, their role as consumers is not nearly as important to them as is their role as producers." [10]

Lack of cohesion on the part of its clientele may also be highly disadvantageous to an administrative agency. Throughout much of its early history, the National Labor Relations Board suffered greatly from the split in the ranks of the trade union movement between the AFL and the CIO. The agency often found itself caught in a cross-fire between the rival labor organizations it was trying to protect even while it was attempting to fend off attacks from employers hostile to its very existence.

It might be assumed ordinarily that as the size of an agency's clientele decreases, its ability to provide the agency with effective support will diminish. This does not, however, need to be the case, since a clientele that is dwindling may become, precisely because it is losing its own position of power in society, even more dependent upon a government agency and the services it provides, and hence more intensely devoted to it. The intensity of commitment of its clientele may thus be no less important to an executive agency than the size and cohesion of its following.

Of course, from the point of view of an administrative agency, there is no clientele worse than one whose members are not included within the American voting population. In its successive incarnations in various organizational forms, the foreign aid agency has been gravely disadvantaged by the fact that it serves foreign groups that do not participate in American elections. The fact that it has been subject to reorganization so many times testifies to the weakness of its support, since agencies like the Corps of Engineers that serve strong clientele groups have generally been able to resist having reorganization imposed on them. In an effort to counter this weakness, the agency's promotional efforts have stressed the fact that many American economic interests benefit from goods produced in this country for eventual shipment overseas as part of foreign aid. In this way the agency seeks to transform its clientele of foreign nationals into an indigenous constituency.

At the opposite extreme is a clientele such as the agricultural population, which has always enjoyed a position of high prestige in American society. The view that Jefferson first articulated has never been seriously challenged in American or for that matter in any other society: "The proportion which the aggregate of the other classes of citizens bears in any State to that of its husbandmen, is the proportion of its unsound to its healthy parts." The most remarkable aspect of this attitude is that it has so strongly persisted even though each decade has seen a steady decline in the size of the farm population.[11]

Certainly the strong position of the Department of Agriculture in American bureaucracy has not been appreciably weakened by this decline. The ability of the department to maintain its strength even in the face of a sharp contraction in the size of its clientele can partially be attributed to the prestigious position of the farmer in American life, and the fact that so many urban residents share the farmers' image of themselves as a chosen people. For many Americans a sentimental tie with the country remained long after they had voted with their feet for urban life by moving to the city.

The structure of a constituency is also important in determining its value to an agency. As noted earlier, an administrative agency that derives most of its support from a single outside group often finds itself excessively dependent upon the group for political support. As a result the group may acquire the power to prevent an agency from pursuing goals that the organization regards as professionally desirable. There is no certainty that the objectives of a bureaucracy will always mesh with the goals of an interest group upon which it depends for political support. Hence, an agency generally prefers to draw its support from a variety of groups, no one of which possesses substantial control over it. Interest groups, on the other hand, favor organizational arrangements that enable them to monopolize rather than share membership in an agency's constituency. Hence, they resist reorganization proposals that would force them to share an agency's attention with other groups.

The term constituency ordinarily includes all groups that perceive themselves or that are perceived by an agency as being affected by its activities. Some of these groups benefit from an agency's work — in this discussion they are referred to as its clientele. For other groups the agency may be a source of penalties or sanctions — they may look upon it with hostility, or even desire its extinction.[12] An agency's power thus rests on a favorable balance of attitudes toward it in the public. It needs not only to win friends but to avoid acquiring enemies. In this respect, regulatory agencies are usually worse off than agencies performing service functions. If it vigorously enforces the law it is charged to administer, a regulatory agency is bound to incur the displeasure of segments of the public upon which it imposes constraints. But if it is insufficiently aggressive in enforcing the law, the groups on whose behalf regulation is being carried on may be peevishly critical of the agency for not doing more to advance their interests, or, as often happens, these friendly groups may leave the agency to fend for itself once it has been established.

A service agency, on the other hand, ordinarily generates benefits rather than restrictions upon the public, and the groups it serves usually constitute a solid core of support for the agency's survival and development. Of course, there are great differentials in constituency support even among such service agencies. Taxpayer opposition to increasing the costs of any program is always possible, and this resistance is not evenly apportioned among all government services. Educational agencies, for example, carry on activities designed to achieve one of the most highly cherished values in American society, and they perform this role for all strata of society. Contrariwise, welfare agencies administer a function that sharply conflicts with the traditional American norm of individual self-reliance, and they perform it for lower income groups that are unorganized, demoralized, and often, as nonwhites, vulnerable to racial prejudice. The socioeconomic status as well as the geographical distribution of a clientele may thus be a strategic factor contributing to its influence.

From this point of view the best situation for any agency is to serve what might be called an "elite" constituency. This may be a group like bankers who stand very high on the socioeconomic ladder. But, since prestige can accrue from occupation as well as social standing or wealth, the elite constituency may also be a professional group in high-status fields like science or medicine. The National Institutes of Health and the National Science Foundation derive much of their strength and standing as government agencies from the prestigious character of the professional clientele with which they interact.

But with respect to any particular administrative function, there may be wide variations in the character of their constituency among different governmental jurisdictions. A school system in a large urban center may be buffeted constantly about by the conflicting demands of different neighborhoods for better services — a tension that is particularly acute today between white and nonwhite segments of the community. In a neighboring suburb, inhabited mainly by well-to-do citizens, the educational system may be at the pinnacle of the administrative pyramid — well financed, the teachers highly paid, and the clientele loyal and devoted to the welfare of the schools.

In summary, it can be said that the ideal administrative constituency from the point of view of an executive agency is large and well distributed throughout all strata of society or in every geographical section of the community. It should include devoted supporters who derive tangible benefit from the services an agency provides. However, an administrative agency should not be excessively dependent upon the support of any segment of the community, nor should it carry on activities that threaten the interests of substantial outside groups. Finally, the economic or social activities in which its clientele engages should be in accord with the most highly ranked values in the society. To the extent that it has these characteristics, an agency's constituency is in a position to give it effective support toward the achievement of its goals.

ORGANIZATIONAL ESPRIT

During the Kennedy administration, no agency of the national government ascended more rapidly into the limelight or more quickly won the esteem of all sections of the community than the Peace Corps. Established in 1961 to help meet the need of the so-called emerging nations for trained manpower, the agency quickly established itself as one of the major successes of the Kennedy years. Talented young men and women whose aspirations would not normally be directed toward the public service flocked to the Peace Corps from all directions in spite of the fact that the remuneration they received was meager and the conditions under which they were expected to work abroad were uncomfortable and often hazardous. To be sure, this kind of organizational élan can be transitory. The attraction of the Peace Corps for young people was an early casualty of American involvement in Vietnam.

But it is nonetheless clear that an agency can derive enormous value from the performance of a function that excites the imagination of the community. In an analysis of the structure and operation of bureaucratic systems, Amitai Etzioni identifies three kinds of power that organizations exercise over their members — coercive, remunerative, and normative.[13] Coercive power is the threat or the actual use of physical control; remunerative control is the use of material rewards as incentives; and normative power rests on the manipulation of "esteem, prestige, and ritualistic symbols."

Looked at from the perspective of this analytical scheme, the Peace Corps was in its heyday a striking illustration of a normative organization in the public service. Its power rested on the enthusiasm it was able to generate for its functions from both those who worked for it and the community at large. It is not, of course, the only example available of a public agency with this kind of appeal. Elite military organizations, with a distinctive tradition and a membership drawn from volunteers rather than conscripts, have traditionally provided the most vivid displays of normative commitment in public bureaucracy. In early periods of American history the Marine Corps generated a great deal of zeal and dedication. The "Green Berets" — a special military force created during the Kennedy administration to deal with the task of combatting guerrilla warfare — had a similar kind of organizational vitality until it was discredited by some of the roles it was called upon to play in Vietnam. The Peace Corps is an unusual demonstration of the capacity of a public agency to ignite enthusiasm without resort to regimental flags, legends of courage, feats of valor, or the other appeals of military life.

Another way to describe the power of an organization like the Peace Corps is to say that it is charismatic, insofar as it evokes a faith and enthusiasm that transcend rational calculation. However, this use of the term "charismatic" differs sharply from that of Max Weber — from whose work the concept of charisma in modern social science is largely derived. In Weber's view, bureaucracy and charisma were antithetical terms. Social movements that began under the leadership of a charismatic leader became bureaucracies as their functions were rationalized and routinized in formal organizations

— the sect in the end became a church. "In its economic substructure, as in everything else," Weber wrote, "charismatic domination is the very opposite of bureaucratic domination." [14]

It is possible to discern within bureaucratic organizations themselves a tendency to move from an initial period of enthusiasm and energy to a subsequent stage when the organization becomes routinized and gradually loses a good deal of its original élan. If this transition cannot, in Weber's terminology, be said to mark an evolution from charisma to bureaucracy, it certainly bears a close resemblance to such a transformation. In his description of the "life cycle" of independent regulatory commissions of the national government, Marver Bernstein shows that once such agencies have gotten past an initial stage of youthful zeal, they undergo a process of devitalization that culminates in old age in a period of debility and decline. "Complacency and inertia appear as inevitable developments in the life cycle of a commission. Although tradition, precedent, and custom can harden into blind routine in all types of social organization, the commission seems to be peculiarly susceptible to the disease of 'administrative arteriosclerosis.' " [15]

This tendency of established organizations to become wedded to routines and resistant to change has frequently been used to justify the creation of new institutions to administer innovative programs. The establishment by President Franklin D. Roosevelt of a variety of "alphabetical" agencies such as the WPA and the CCC in the early 1930s has been widely interpreted as a step on his part to insure that New Deal programs would be carried on with vigor and enthusiasm, rather than being smothered in the red tape and lassitude with which existing agencies would approach their administration.

As far as Roosevelt was concerned, this problem presented itself in a particularly acute form in the case of the Department of Agriculture. Before Roosevelt's time, the department was strongly committed to a philosophy of confining the national role in agriculture to educational activities channeled through the state extension agencies. The new programs Roosevelt contemplated involved a direct relationship between the national government and the farmer in such fields as rural electrification and soil conservation. Faced with this dilemma, Roosevelt's characteristically diplomatic solution was to establish his programs initially in independent agencies such as the Rural Electrification Administration and the

Soil Conservation Service. Then, as these agencies gained sufficient administrative experience and outside political support to insure their viability, he allowed them to be incorporated into the department. By this time the agencies were too strong for the department to sabotage their mission. Indeed, there was on the contrary reasonable expectation that the agencies might infuse the department with their own more aggressive attitude toward agricultural administration.[16]

Organizational esprit depends to a large extent upon the development of an appropriate ideology or sense of mission on the part of an administrative agency both as a method of binding outside supporters to the agency and as a technique for intensifying the loyalty of the organization's employees to its purposes. Some of the conservation agencies have developed almost a mystical sense of mission about their function in the administrative apparatus — the preservation of some priceless asset such as the forests, the soil, natural beauty, or historic monuments. This ideology is a powerful force not only in maintaining the esprit of conservation agencies, but also in heightening their impact upon the development of public policy.

Of course, not all agencies perform functions that allow them to develop either a persuasive ideology or a sense of esprit. Any agency may seek through public relations activity to "glamorize" its role, but wholly artificial esprit is difficult to sustain. A great many agencies have a forceful sense of mission early in their history, but tend to lose this crusading spirit as they mature. A few agencies have managed to sustain it throughout much of their history, and cases of administrative renaissance are not entirely unknown. But where enthusiastic performance is sought for in the public service, the common practice has been to create new agencies in order to achieve it. This is one of many reasons why bureaucracies tend to multiply.

While public organizations are subject to decline, it is noteworthy that such organizations rarely die. If nothing else, an agency provides a livelihood for its employees and a cluster of outside interests aggregate around its functions and support their continuance. Certainly, as compared to private organizations, public agencies have a very low mortality rate. Indeed, some failing private organizations — colleges and museums, for example — are taken over by the government and given a new lease on life as public institutions. Even though critics of bureaucracy often feel that there are many government agencies that should declare bankruptcy, there is no record of any agency actually doing so, and going out of business.

More commonly, what occurs in the case of a devitalized public agency is not death but resurrection. A change in the political climate suddenly gives new life to its dormant functions. The U.S. Employment Service, after playing a very active role in World War I in finding workers for war industries, went into a state of something resembling suspended animation in the 1920s. But with the collapse of the economy and the depression of the 1930s, the employment service became an extremely important part of the Roosevelt administration's attack on poverty.

Faced with threats to their survival, public agencies often change their functions or adapt the way in which they perform their traditional tasks. Under criticism from consumer groups that felt the agency had been captured by the business interests it was supposed to regulate, the Federal Trade Commission began in the 1970s to be much more vigorous in enforcing consumer protection legislation. During the same period, the Corps of Engineers, under heavy fire for neglecting environmental interests in its water resource projects, began to exhibit at least the appearance of being much more environmentally conscious in planning and operating its dams and other facilities.

ADMINISTRATIVE STATECRAFT

The role of leadership in shaping the success of any organization is as elusive as it is important. On frequent occasions the ability of an administrative agency to achieve its goals and to secure the resources necessary for its survival depends directly on the identity of its leader. Early in the Truman administration, Congress made it very clear that the Federal Security Agency would never obtain the status of an executive department as long as Oscar Ewing was at the head of the agency. When Eisenhower became president, and Ewing was succeeded by Oveta Culp Hobby, the proposal to transform the FSA into the Department of Health, Education, and Welfare quickly won congressional approval.

The story of Jesse Jones as secretary of commerce provides equally impressive evidence of the importance of leadership to an organization. During Jones's tenure as commerce secretary, his ability to command support in Congress and devoted allegiance from the business community was legendary. When Roosevelt removed Jones and appointed Henry A. Wallace as secretary of commerce in 1945, Congress immediately proceeded to remove from the department one of its most important constituent bureaus — the Reconstruction Finance Corporation. And the decisive factor in bringing about this reduction in the scope of the department's jurisdiction was the replacement of Jones by Wallace.[17] Thus, personal antagonisms that its executive generates may be extremely costly to an administrative organization.

Of course, in appraising the role of leadership in an administrative agency, it should be recognized that leadership in public administration, like leadership in any organizational context, is to a large extent situational — dependent, that is, on factors in the environment other than the leader himself. Jones was successful as secretary of commerce in large part because his department served a business constituency that was strong in Congress, and still very powerful in the outside community, but that looked upon Jones as its only real protagonist in the executive branch. The influence Jones exercised was thus a product not only of his own capacities but of the circumstances that prevailed when he was in office. For the conservatives in Congress and the country, Jones was a solid and sensible figure in an otherwise radical administration. For President Roosevelt, Jones was a natural bridge to a constituency in which his administration was generally very weak. Jones's personal attributes thus fit perfectly the role he was called upon to play. He would have been far less successful as secretary of labor than he was as secretary of commerce, since none of his skills could have overcome easily the hostility in Congress and the business community toward the Department of Labor.

During the Kennedy administration Sargent Shriver was widely heralded as the model of successful leadership while he was head of the Peace Corps, and many newspaper accounts appeared celebrating the dexterity with which he handled relations with Congress and the public in advancing the cause of the agency over which he presided. However, after Johnson became president, Shriver took over responsibility for the Office of Economic Opportunity — an agency established to carry on "the war against poverty" in the United States. This assignment produced very little in the way of adulatory comment. But the presumption is strong that Shriver was no less able a leader in the Office of Economic Opportunity than he was in the Peace Corps. The critical change that occurred was in the nature of his assignment — from an agency carrying on generally popular activities abroad that did not threaten any important interests in the United States to an agency caught in the turbulence of racial conflict and welfare politics in major American cities.

In short, while an institution is often described as the lengthened shadow of a man, it may be equally correct to say that an executive is the lengthened shadow of an institution, since his own prestige may largely reflect the appeal of the organization he commands. Consequently, an executive who values his reputation as a leader must choose well the institution in which he exercises his talents — to make certain that there is a match between his abilities and the institution's needs. Or better yet, an institution can be one of those rare organizations that so well meets the mood of its time that it is assured of success. But in the end an administrative executive, like Machiavelli's Prince, cannot escape the impact of chance upon the success of his career — being in the right place, at the right time, with the right tactic. As Machiavelli described the fate of leadership: "men are successful while they are in close harmony with Fortune, and when they are out of harmony, they are unsuccessful." [18]

Perhaps no executive career in recent years rose or fell more steeply than that of Robert MacNamara, secretary of defense for both Presidents Kennedy and Johnson. Under Kennedy and in his early service with Johnson, MacNamara was the very model of the modern executive — highly knowledgeable, sure of his decisions, and conveying an air of competence that overawed his opponents. But as the Vietnam War worked its inexorable way toward the top of the department's agenda and public attention, MacNamara found himself in charge of a failure, whether of his own contrivance or not made little difference. His reputation waned steadily, and by the time he resigned there was very little left of the original radiance of his image. Never was the power of Machiavelli's "fortuna" better exemplified.

But when this much has been said about the accidental factors that help to determine the success of leadership, it is nonetheless true that executives in quite similar positions in public bureaucracy often have varying degrees of success at their jobs. It seems reasonable to conclude, therefore, that the capacities of a leader can make a difference to an administrative agency and that there are certain skills associated with the effective performance of the executive role in an administrative organization that can be identified as contributing to a leader's success.

Leadership skills in the context of public bureaucracy are of principal value in two areas of an executive's responsibility: (1) externally, in insuring a favorable response to the agency from the outside groups and organizations that control resources upon which it depends; (2) internally, in maintaining the morale of employees of the agency and their commitment to its goals. In large organizations, these external and internal responsibilities of leadership are so complex and demanding that they customarily require considerable specialization, and the organization is in effect run by an executive cabinet in which some individuals are given responsibility for handling external relations, while the duties of others relate primarily to the internal functioning of the institution. However, even under this cabinet system, the head of an agency retains responsibility for the success or failure of the organization, as well as the privilege of choosing his executive associates and of deciding which of his responsibilities he will delegate and to whom.

As far as the external responsibilities of leadership are concerned, all studies of this subject stress the importance of an executive's ability to create confidence in his own personal and technical capacities among those who control resources the agency needs. The executive must be in some sense a "trusted leader" upon whom others can rely. Fenno's work on the appropriations process suggests that the willingness of Congress to grant an agency the funds it needs to carry on its work is very much determined by the confidence legislators have in the head of the organization.[19]

What an agency head needs to know, therefore, is what techniques will help instill confidence in his abilities within his constituency. On this subject we have some guidelines especially in the area of an executive's relations with legislators — a key elite with which the heads of public agencies normally deal. Studies in this field agree that at appropriations hearings and in other contacts with lawmakers, the head of an agency should display such qualities as honesty and clarity in the presentation of his agency's needs, a passion for economy in the use of public funds, and simplicity and affability of manner in personal contacts.[20]

In executive legislative relations, it is essential for an agency executive to recognize that congressmen are in a highly vulnerable political position, subject as they are to removal from office by defeat at the polls. For a legislator, survival depends upon maintaining good relations with his constituents. This is why so many congressmen give top priority to their *ombudsman* role — helping constituents handle problems they have with the federal government. The least the head of any agency can do is to avoid, whenever possible, decisions and actions by his agency that may be embarrassing to a congressman in his own district. On the more positive side, he can take steps to lend the congressman certain forms of political support. The agency can routinely provide help and information in handling questions that constituents bring to a congressman, or it may help a congressman advertise himself by arranging for a well-publicized trip to a field installation, or by allowing him to announce from his office the negotiation of a government contract, or the establishment of an administrative facility that will redound to his credit in his district. If reciprocity is the unwritten if not altogether inviolable law of political life, an executive can reasonably expect that these investments will bring a high rate of political return.

As important as any skill an executive may possess is an ability to communicate successfully with his constituency. Very often the language in which administrative policies are explained and defended is as important to their success as the policies themselves. In the field of higher education, for example, state university officials have frequently demonstrated great skill in the use of metaphors that will bring the distinctive needs of higher learning home to their agricultural constituencies. In a celebrated defense of academic freedom, the regents of the University of Wisconsin stressed their belief that "the great State University of Wisconsin should ever encourage that continual and fearless *sifting and winnowing* by which alone the truth can be found" (italics supplied). A similar sensitivity to the importance of using appropriate language in addressing a constituency was displayed in Texas where, in protesting efforts to force the university to spend money from its reserve fund, an administrator vehemently declared that this policy would deprive the school of its "seed-corn." [21]

In dealing with their various publics it is important that executives not only have the qualities associated with leadership but that they display these qualities as dramatically as possible. Victor Thompson has stressed the importance of dramaturgy to the effective performance of the leader's role.[22] Successful executives must be skilled in impression management — the ability to convey to others a sense of their own capacities. State university presidents have in recent years concerned themselves not only with being more efficient but also with convincing others that they are running an efficient institution:

> . . . it is of vital importance that the state legislature and the taxpaying public . . . be convinced of the soundness of university operations. Under the pressures of competition from other state institutions, a large state university is often forced to put on a dramatic show of scientific objectivity in order to justify its requests for continued support, even though the dramatic props — elaborate formulas, statistical ratios, and so on — may have very little to do with the way in which decisions are actually made within the academic establishment. As one administrative vice-president remarked about the preparation of the university budget, "We simply use the displays that give us the best image. . . ."[23]

As they have developed in recent years in higher education, techniques of scientific management may thus serve not so much to manage the university as to manage the impression that outsiders have about the university.

External relations occupy a good deal of the time and attention of the head of any administrative agency. Just as the duties of the president of the United States have increasingly come to center on foreign affairs, so executives in public agencies find themselves drawn increasingly into community relations activity, negotiations with other organizations, and a variety of other roles that involve the interaction between their organization and its environment. In the words of Herbert Simon:

> Observation indicates that, as the higher levels are approached in administrative organizations, the administrator's "internal" task (his relations with the organization subordinate to him) decreases in importance relative to his "external" task (his relations with persons outside the organization). An ever

larger part of his work may be subsumed under the heads of
"public relations" and "promotion." [24]

But if external relations have become dominant in the performance of the executive role, internal responsibilities have by no
means disappeared. Apart from attending to the purely housekeeping chores of management, an executive has such major internal
responsibilities as arousing the enthusiasm and the energy of the
organization's employees for its objectives, settling disputes and
conflicts of interest within the organization, and generally serving
as a catalytic agent for the continuous appraisal of existing programs, and the inauguration, whenever necessary, of innovations in
policy.

Very often these external and internal responsibilities tend to
pull an executive in opposite directions. Decisions he makes to
maintain harmony with the outside world may alienate the organization's employees. Conversely, the employees of an agency may
push an executive in directions that make it more difficult to maintain good relations with outside groups. While he was secretary of
state, Dean Acheson was a staunch defender of Department of State
employees against attacks on their loyalty in Congress — a position
that did little to endear him in influential circles of the legislature.
On the other hand, his successor, John Foster Dulles, improved his
relations with Congress by taking certain steps to tighten security
procedures in the department. Since some of these steps were regarded as detrimental to their interests by Department of State employees, Dulles improved the department's external image at the
price of seriously weakening his own standing with its staff.[25]

His relationship with the White House generates especially
strong cross-pressures upon the head of an executive agency in the
United States. A president expects loyalty from agency executives
both to himself personally and to his programs. This expectation
may put the executive on the horns of a dilemma if the president's
policies are unpopular with either the agency's employees or its
constituents. They may expect instead that the executive will become a protagonist of their goals and objectives, even if this means
alienating the White House.

Two of President Nixon's appointees lost their Cabinet seats as
a result of these cross-pressures. Secretary of Health, Education, and
Welfare Robert Finch found himself caught between White House

expectations that he would help bring about a reduction in the scale of welfare expenditures and the strong view within the department that these programs should not be scuttled. As a result of this and other issues, the polarization between the White House and the agency became acute, and Finch resigned, escaping by his departure a face-to-face meeting with aroused departmental employees. A similar kind of conflict led the White House to demand the resignation of Walter Hickel as secretary of the interior.

Moreover, hard choices confront an executive in the day-to-day management of his agency — the need to balance uncertain gains against certain losses, or perhaps to choose the lesser of two evils in a context in which the question of which is the lesser evil is precisely the issue in doubt. In the case of national agencies, an executive is confronted by a board of directors in the form of a congressional committee that has many members who — for partisan reasons — wish him ill rather than well. The president whom he nominally serves may well abandon him if he gets into trouble. The agency's employees are career bureaucrats who may choose to ignore or defy him, and who cannot easily be disciplined or dismissed. It is in this refractory environment that administrative statecraft must be carried on in the public service, and what is perhaps most remarkable is not that many fail, but that some succeed.

THE PURSUIT OF POWER

If the sources of administrative power are varied, so too are the motives that animate administrative agencies in their quest for primacy. Most clearly apparent is the desire of agencies to strengthen their position in order to enhance their ability to achieve such manifest goals as better medical care, a more effective system of crime control, or the prevention of water pollution. The statutory objectives of public agencies today are wide-ranging, and in order to fulfill its mission, every agency requires an adequate supply of resources to employ personnel and meet the other expenses of organizational life. These resources are easier for the strong to obtain than the weak, so power is sought not for its own sake but because it is an essential prerequisite for carrying on an effective program.

But along with these manifest goals by which agencies are inspired in their quest for power, certain other latent objectives are also commonly present. At the upper reaches of the hierarchy, agency executives may have a strong desire for power as a means of gratifying a personal need for status and the other perquisites of office. On the part of rank-and-file personnel, the pursuit of power may be primarily designed to insure the continuation of certain more tangible rewards that are important to them as civil servants, including adequate salaries, pensions, working conditions, and fringe benefits. The preservation and improvement of these remunerative incentives have become the special responsibility of public employee organizations.[26]

These varied motives for which power is sought are not, of course, necessarily incompatible. An agency may be most capable of serving the public interest when it is led by an ambitious chief executive, who may, while using the agency as a springboard for advancing his own career, bring it to new levels of achievement in its capacity for public service. A private vice can, as Adam Smith long ago noted, often be transformed into a public virtue. The community may also be as well served if rank-and-file employees are allowed to gratify their continuing desire for improvements in remuneration and working conditions. It is certainly reasonable to expect that satisfied employees will be more efficient than those who cherish grievances. Public and private interests may thus dovetail neatly together, in the best of all possible administrative worlds.

There are, however, other less attractive possibilities. The personal goals of agency employees may gain a distinct priority over the actual purposes for which an organization was created. Public organizations and officials are often in a position to justify their pursuit of power on the basis of disinterested criteria like service to the public, when in fact power is sought only to advance the selfish interests of the organization's members. A general may launch a military campaign during a war at great cost to the lives of his own troops, which will contribute very little to the fortunes of his country but a great deal to the success of his own career. Staff members of any organization may push for the adoption of policies that reflect not the needs of any significant segment of the public they service, but their own desire for power, prestige, or security. In this category are pessimistic assessments by the armed forces of a potential enemy's capabilities or intentions that are contrived in order to pressure the public into supporting an expansion in the strength of the military.

This kind of distortion occurs in its most flagrant form in cases of administrative corruption, where some members of a law enforcement agency may look upon its power not as a means of protecting the safety of the public, but as an instrument for extorting tribute from the individuals engaged in the illegal activity they are supposed to be suppressing. In situations of this kind, the needs of the public recede altogether, and administrative power is used merely to advance the private goals of agency employees.

Of course, the private interests that members of an administrative agency serve need not necessarily be their own. As noted earlier, there are many public agencies that, either in their initial establishment or eventual development, exist mainly as satellite organizations for outside groups. A licensing board, for example, may be set up for the manifest public purpose of insuring that certain professional standards are adhered to in the practice of a particular skill. But in actual fact the latent function of such an agency may be that of limiting entry into the profession to protect the economic position of present members of the group, thus inflicting costs upon the public it is supposed to serve.

Whatever its motives may be in seeking greater authority, an agency must constantly reckon with the fact that an expansion in jurisdiction does not always result in an expansion of power. While bureaucracies are often pictured as being implacably imperialist in their desire to expand their jurisdiction, in actual fact there are occasions when an agency may increase its power by narrowing, or refusing to expand, the scope of its legal authority. According to Wallace S. Sayre and Herbert Kaufman, for example, the agencies in New York City's government

> . . . compete to avoid program assignments that are especially difficult and controversial. The Commissioner of Hospitals and the Commissioner of Correction have both tried to prevent lodging responsibility for treatment of narcotics addicts in their departments, and the Department of Health has been restive under burdens of building inspection the Commissioner and the Board of Health would generally prefer to have placed entirely on the Department of Buildings.[27]

Thus, in the quest for power an agency's strategy has to be one of optimizing rather than maximizing its jurisdiction. Activities that have weak political support, are inordinately expensive, or that divert an agency from its essential purposes may represent liabilities rather than assets from the point of view of an agency's power balance.

Sometimes the most significant limitation upon an agency's ability to grow comes not from external forces but from its own image of itself — its sense of its proper mission. In the United States the State Department has allowed other agencies to expand and occupy territory in the foreign affairs field largely because the foreign service professionals who dominate the department take a narrow view of their role — confining it to diplomacy and excluding such matters as scientific research and economic forecasting that have become increasingly relevant to foreign policy.[28] The Defense Department, on the other hand, has been much more willing to recruit professionals in areas other than the military, or to retrain military officers in order to protect its hegemony over the resolution of national security issues that increasingly turn on expertise in science and technology.

Perhaps the most embarrassing kind of jurisdiction an agency can acquire is control over an activity that is anathema either to its own sense of what its mission is or to its constituency. This was the unhappy fate of the Department of Labor in 1963, when it was put in charge of administering the Landrum-Griffin Act, a statute designed to protect union members from abuses of power by their own officers. Prior to its enactment this legislation had been bitterly fought by the labor organizations that represent the department's chief source of outside support, and since 1963 the Department of Labor has discharged its responsibilities in this area with a notable lack of enthusiasm.[29] In cases of this kind, administration of the law may become in fact nullification of the law, or as some would put it, sabotage of its intent.

It should be borne in mind that executive agencies, like all contestants in the struggle for power, operate with imperfect knowledge regarding the kind of strategy that will advance their interests. An agency may, for example, strongly resist measures that it feels will reduce its authority, only to find, when the changes actually take place, that no such effects have occurred. In advancing or protecting its power interests, as on other matters, an executive agency thus operates within the limits of what Herbert Simon calls "bounded rationality." [30] The course of action best calculated to achieve its objectives is not always clear to it.

Notes

1. Norton Long, *The Polity* (Chicago: Rand McNally & Co., 1962), p. 50.
2. See Robert A. Dahl, *Modern Political Analysis* (Englewood Cliffs, N.J.: Prentice-Hall, 1970), pp. 39–54.
3. Burton R. Clark, "Organizational Adaptation and Precarious Values: A Case Study," *American Sociological Review* 21 (June 1956): 327–36.
4. Ibid., p. 335.
5. Edward Feit, *The Armed Bureaucrats* (Boston: Houghton Mifflin Co., 1973).
6. See Lucian W. Pye, *Aspects of Political Development* (Boston: Little, Brown and Co., 1966), pp. 172–87.
7. For an argument that scientists are in some sense a new "power elite," see Don K. Price, *The Scientific Estate* (Cambridge: Harvard University Press, 1965), and Ralph E. Lapp, *The New Priesthood* (New York: Harper and Row, 1965). Cf. also, however, the searching critique of this elitist thesis by Daniel S. Greenberg, "The Myth of the Scientific Elite," *The Public Interest* 1 (Fall 1965): 51–62.
8. Cf. the discussion of this point in Harold L. Wilensky, *Organizational Intelligence* (New York: Basic Books, Inc., 1967), pp. 106–7. The standing of economists has slipped somewhat in recent years as a result of their difficulty in providing government with effective solutions to the problem of inflation and recession.
9. Arthur Maass, *Muddy Waters* (Cambridge: Harvard University Press, 1951).
10. Mark V. Nadel, "Unorganized Interests and the Politics of Consumer Protection," in Michael P. Smith and Associates, *Politics in America* (New York: Random House, 1974), p. 149.
11. The literature bearing on this point is extensive. See, for example, Richard Hofstadter, *The Age of Reform* (New York: Alfred A. Knopf, 1955), Henry Nash Smith, *Virgin Land* (Cambridge: Harvard University Press, 1950), and Leo Marx, *Machine in the Garden* (New York: Oxford University Press, 1964).
12. Cf. Matthew Holden, Jr., " 'Imperialism' in Bureaucracy," *American Political Science Review* LX (December 1966): 944. In Holden's view, the constituency of any agency head includes "those who support his ends, those who oppose his ends, and those who wish to intervene for what he regards as 'irrelevant' purposes." Holden also looks upon groups of employees within the agency as "internal constituencies" from the point of view of an agency executive. Murray Edelman, on the other hand, defines administrative constituencies as "the groups which have the power to remove the incumbents or kill the organization if it does not respond to their wishes." See "Governmental Organization and Public Policy," *Public Administration Review* XII

(Autumn 1952): 277. Unfortunately, from their point of view, not many groups served by an administrative agency actually have the power "to kill the organization if it does not respond to their wishes," though they can certainly devitalize it by withdrawing their support.

13. See Amitai Etzioni, *A Comparative Analysis of Complex Organizations* (New York: Free Press of Glencoe, 1961).

14. See H. H. Gerth and C. Wright Mills, eds., *From Max Weber: Essays in Sociology* (New York: Oxford University Press, 1946), p. 247.

15. Marver H. Bernstein, *Regulating Business by Independent Commission* (Princeton, N.J.: Princeton University Press, 1955), p. 101.

16. An analysis of Roosevelt's strategy with respect to administrative organization may be found in Arthur Schlesinger, Jr., *The Coming of the New Deal* (Boston: Houghton Mifflin Co., 1959), pp. 533–52.

17. For a brief but enlightening analysis of Jones's career as secretary of commerce, see Richard F. Fenno, *The President's Cabinet* (Cambridge: Harvard University Press, 1959), pp. 234–47.

18. See *The Prince* in Machiavelli, *The Chief Works and Others*, trans. Allan Gilbert (Durham, N.C.: Duke University Press, 1965), I: 92.

19. Richard F. Fenno, *The Power of the Purse* (Boston: Little, Brown and Co., 1966), pp. 288–91.

20. See, in this regard, ibid., pp. 285–91, and Aaron Wildavsky, *The Politics of the Budgetary Process* (Boston: Little, Brown and Co., 1974), pp. 74–84.

21. Malcolm Moos and Francis E. Rourke, *The Campus and the State* (Baltimore: The Johns Hopkins Press, 1959), pp. 24–25.

22. See Victor A. Thompson, *Modern Organization* (New York: Alfred A. Knopf, 1961), pp. 138–51.

23. See Francis E. Rourke and Glenn E. Brooks, "The 'Managerial Revolution' in Higher Education," *Administrative Science Quarterly* 9 (September 1964): 180–81.

24. Herbert A. Simon, *Administrative Behavior* (New York: Macmillan, 2nd ed., 1957), p. 217.

25. See, in this regard, Norman A. Graebner, ed., *An Uncertain Tradition: American Secretaries of State in the Twentieth Century* (New York: McGraw-Hill, 1961), pp. 267–308.

26. The divergence between the goals of individuals and the goals of the organizations of which they are members is a recurring theme in organization theory. See especially the work of Chris Argyris, *Personality and Organization: The Conflict Between System and the Individual* (New York: Harper, 1957), and *Interpersonal Competence and Organizational Effectiveness* (Homewood, Ill.: Dorsey Press, 1962).

27. Wallace S. Sayre and Herbert Kaufman, *Governing New York City* (New York: Russell Sage Foundation, 1960), p. 262.

28. See Andrew M. Scott, "Environmental Change and Organizational Adaptation," *International Studies Quarterly* 14 (March 1970): 85–94, and John E. Haar, *The Professional Diplomat* (Princeton, N.J.: Princeton University Press, 1969).

29. A similar case involving the failure of the Federal Power Commission to enforce the Natural Gas Act is cited by Holden, "'Imperialism,'" p. 945.

30. See Herbert Simon, *Models of Man* (New York: John Wiley & Sons, 1957), pp. 196–206.

Part Two

BUREAUCRACY AND PUBLIC POLICY

CHAPTER FIVE

The Policy
Process in
Bureaucracy

The preceding chapters have examined some of the principal reasons why administrative agencies now play so large a role in the political system. The basic resources upon which administrative power has been shown to depend are the possession of a skill essential to reaching decisions in vital areas of policy and the ability to mobilize an influential constituency. Both knowledge and politics are major sources of bureaucratic power. An agency's ability to exert influence in the policy process can also be traced to the esprit or vitality of the organization and the extent to which it is effectively led. In the more powerful administrative organizations, such as the Federal Bureau of Investigation in its heyday, a position of influence tends to reflect the simultaneous presence of all these factors — a valued skill, strong public support, organizational esprit, and adroit leadership.

In this chapter we begin a consideration of some of the essential characteristics of the policy-making process within bureaucracy. Two aspects of this process deserve particular attention in an analysis of the forces and factors that shape the outcome of deliberations on policy issues within administrative agencies. The first is the identity of the principal groups in administrative agencies that participate in the development of policy. Here we confront what might be called the internal politics of bureaucracy, in the sense of conflict among individuals playing different parts inside executive agencies. This system of internal politics does as much to shape the structure of policy as the interaction between agencies and outside groups and organizations. Much of it is hidden from public view and only becomes visible when conflict becomes intense and "boils over," as participants who are losing out in the internal struggle leak information to the outside world in an effort to draw public attention to the dispute and change the outcome in their favor.

The second question at the focus of concern is the nature of the policy process within administrative agencies. How does policy-making change and what are its distinctive characteristics when its center of gravity shifts from legislative assemblies to the corridors of bureaucracy? This chapter considers some of the significant ways in which the policy-making process in executive agencies is shaped by the fact that it is being carried on within a bureaucratic environment.

PARTICIPANTS IN BUREAUCRATIC POLICY-MAKING

In much of the literature and folklore about bureaucracy, the image that emerges is one of unity in structure and uniformity in perspective. Generalizations about the bureaucrat and the administrative role in government often seem to assume a total homogeneity in outlook on the part of all those working in executive agencies. By outside observers, the word most often used to describe bureaucratic organizations is "monolithic."

Viewed from within, however, a far different picture emerges. A government agency, like any large and complex organization, can be seen to embrace a variety of points of view that produce diversity in perspective and often generate sharp disputes within the inner councils of the agency. Like a family or any other social organization that radiates an image of togetherness to the outside world, an executive agency shows itself upon close inspection to be far from uniform in the attitudes and behavior of its members.

More specifically there are no less than four cleavages in the ranks of bureaucracy that are central factors in the development of policy within administrative agencies. In the first place, there is commonly a sharp difference in the role and attitude of political appointees at the top of the administrative pyramid and the career administrators beneath them. Second, within the ranks of career employees themselves there is frequently a wide divergence in outlook between the professionals who employ the skills with which the organization serves the community, and the administrators whose chief function is that of maintaining the organization in existence. Third, there is a possibility for "lateral entrance" into an agency's policy deliberations on the part of outside experts who play an advisory or consultative role, or, even for temporary periods, may serve in a full-time capacity with the agency. These outsiders commonly represent a quite distinctive force in the framing of bureaucratic policy. Finally, and apart from the varying roles that officials play within bureaucracy, there are differences in personality or psychological orientation toward their work that promote diversity among bureaucrats.

Political Executives and the Career Staff. A relationship that is fundamental to the determination of policy in any governmental bureaucracy is the interaction between political executives at the top of the administrative pyramid and career officials subordinate to them. In a democratic state the political executive usually represents the political party that has been victorious at the polls. In nondemocratic societies he represents the ruling group that has taken power and presides over the destinies of the state. And in both democratic and nondemocratic states a certain measure of tension and difficulty is a continuing characteristic of relations between career and political cadres.

The traditional interpretation of the relationship between the political and the career administrator stresses the superior influence of the career official upon policy decisions. Max Weber, for example, contends that "the absolute monarch is powerless opposite the superior knowledge of the bureaucratic expert — in a certain sense more powerless than any other political head. . . . The Russian czar of the old regime was seldom able to accomplish permanently anything that displeased his bureaucracy and hurt the power interests of the bureaucrats." [1] A similar view was expressed by John Stuart Mill: "Where everything is done through the bureaucracy, nothing to which the bureaucracy is really adverse can be done at all." [2]

In American bureaucracy, however, the relationship between political and bureaucratic officials is far more subtle and complex than the comments of either Weber or Mill might suggest. While the career official has certain advantages in this relationship, including continuity in office and a greater familiarity with the work of the agency, the political executive is far from powerless. For one thing he presides over a hierarchical system in which his office is a primary source of legitimate authority. Consequently, there is a strong tendency for career bureaucrats to tailor their recommendations to fit what they believe to be his views on policy. And once he has made up his mind on a policy question, these officials will ordinarily support his decision, even if they disagree with it. Cases where career subordinates openly repudiate the decisions of their political superiors often receive great publicity, but they are exceptions to the general willingness of bureaucrats to go along with policies decided upon at a higher level.

During the first term of the Nixon administration, there were several episodes involving public denunciation of official policy by organized groups of career civil servants. The War in Vietnam was the chief target of this bureaucratic rebellion, but other Nixon policies also came under attack — including a cut-back in domestic welfare programs and an apparent weakening in the administration's commitment to vigorous enforcement of civil rights legislation. The protest movement was centered in the Department of Health, Education, and Welfare, but spread to other national agencies as well. This kind of bureaucratic defiance seemed part of a more general rise in political disaffection during the period when the United States was directly involved in the Vietnam hostilities, but it never involved more than 2 percent of all federal employees in Washington.[3]

It is more usual for bureaucratic opposition to official policy to be covert rather than open — guerrilla warfare rather than a frontal assault. Career officials will confide their doubts regarding the wisdom of the policies being followed by their political superiors to friendly congressmen or reporters, or they may alert pressure groups with which they have an intimate relationship to the fact that steps being undertaken are adverse to their interests. They thus convert disputes with political executives into conflicts between their superiors and outside organizations. In this way, they can pursue their objectives without jeopardy to the forms of bureaucratic life or the safety of their own position. Moreover, by avoiding an open break with their superior, they can continue to pass ammunition to his critics from the security of their intimate participation in the affairs and deliberations of the agency. In this surreptitious way, career officials can incite political conflict in the outside world without risking their own safety by direct participation in the combat.

Such warfare is not a frequent occurrence. More commonly, the relationship between political executives and career officials can be described in Charles E. Lindblom's term, as one of "mutual accommodation." [4] Career subordinates have good reason for deferring to their political superior. As already noted, he is invested with the authority of office in a bureaucratic environment in which rank is an impressive symbol of power. Congressmen may be prepared to treat departmental executives with familiarity if not contempt. Ordinary bureaucrats are not.

Second, the political executive, whether elected or appointed, is in some sense a symbol of public control of the governmental process. In a society highly impregnated with democratic ideology — as is true of the United States, for example — this is a formidable source of authority. Finally, in addition to representing the authority of the community in the agency, the political executive also represents the agency in the community. Bureaucrats cannot publicly undermine him without risking injury to the organization with which their personal fortunes are linked. He is the best salesman they have for the achievement of the agency's goals and the continued replenishment of its resources.

At the same time, political executives cannot run roughshod over the views of their career subordinates. While they may be able to coerce these subordinates into obedience, they certainly cannot force them into the enthusiastic performance of their duties, which is essential if the agency is to attain a high level of effectiveness. Moreover, the capacity of career subordinates to make trouble for the executives in the outside community is, as has been suggested, not insubstantial, and this threat also calls for the exercise of diplomacy by the political executive in his dealings with these officials. Such diplomacy may sometimes lead a chief executive to call for improvements in salary and fringe benefits for his staff as a means of purchasing their support for his own policy goals.[5]

In the formal theory of public administration, the role of the career staff is regarded as primarily that of insuring competence in the design of policy — the techniques used to achieve goals should be the most effective available. In actual practice, however, the career staff also tends to develop a fine sensitivity to the political pressures to which an agency is subject. A political executive's best advice on how to operate politically may well come from his career subordinates. They know their way around the political thickets that surround the agency; he does not. Moreover, legislators tend to seek advice on policy questions from career officials, since they often regard these officials as more knowledgeable and trustworthy than political executives.

On the other hand, it is not infrequent in the United States for the politically appointed head of an executive agency to have at least as much if not more competence in the agency's area of expertise than his own career staff. This is especially true in the case of agencies like the National Science Foundation, where outside professional groups insist on the appointment of a top executive with first-rate scientific credentials. In situations of this sort, a political appointee is expected to play a leading role in policy development, while the career officials help him avoid political pitfalls in his dealings with the community, Congress, and other executive agencies.

In democratic societies at least, it has traditionally been assumed that public policy should reflect both the needs and desires of citizens, and the application of the best expert advice and technical skill in satisfying these aspirations. The conventional wisdom has been that the role of reflecting popular preferences should be played by political executives, while career civil servants provide whatever expertise is needed to achieve policy goals. This is the arrangement to be found in British and other parliamentary governments, and it has been endorsed in a number of proposals for reforming the American system. As has been indicated, however, bureaucracy in the United States tends not to follow this neat division of labor. Career officials are often astute politicians and political executives may have impressive credentials as experts. But it has certainly not been demonstrated that policy decisions in American bureaucracy are any less responsive or less competent because the actors involved do not always play the roles assigned to them in traditional democratic theory.

The steady expansion of unionization that has taken place in the public service in recent years has had a growing impact on the relations between political executives and career civil servants. The attention of trade unions is focused on matters related to the "bread and butter" concerns of civil servants — wages, working conditions, fringe benefits, etc. But their power reaches into areas of public policy and executive decision-making as well. Unions in New York City have fought the efforts of civil rights organizations to restructure the organization and procedures of various agencies so as to make them more responsive to the needs of minority groups.[6]

As this union power continues to grow — in national as well as state and local government — it will tend to narrow the authority of political executives over career civil servants, and to create situations in which union members have a dual and sometimes conflicting loyalty to the department for which they work and the union to which they belong. Strikes, slow-downs, and other techniques available to trade unions represent forms of bureaucratic power that loom increasingly large on the landscape of American politics. This is particularly true in metropolitan areas, where a congested population and a dependence upon governmental services make the political system particularly vulnerable to union pressures.

Professionals and Administrators. In a growing number of organizations, in the public service as well as in private life, an increasingly strategic role is being assumed by so-called professional employees — individuals with highly developed skills whose commitment to an organization arises essentially from the fact that it gives them an opportunity to practice their specialized craft.[7] Their primary loyalty remains, however, to their own profession, not to the organization, and their attitudes on many questions are formed by and sometimes peculiar to their particular discipline. Many professions in the public service — city planners, foresters, social workers, and others — have a distinctive ideology with respect to policy in their own area of concern that springs from a deeply rooted tradition of looking at problems in a certain way.

City planners, for example, have a profound commitment to the importance of a city's having a comprehensive design for its own development to which specific proposals for urban land use can be related. Social workers often have a similar attitude of dedication toward the necessity of taking care of the poor and underprivileged in society — an attitude that, at least in its intensity, sets them apart from other groups in bureaucracy. Foresters, like other conservationists, have an almost mystical reverence for the natural resources under their jurisdiction. A founding father of a profession, such as Gifford Pinchot in the case of forestry, may have a place of honor in its development not unlike that of the first patriarch of a religion. Like a religious sect, a profession may also have its hallowed martyrs. Billy Mitchell, in the case of the air force, is one notable example. J. Robert Oppenheimer, in the case of the scientific community, is another.

There is, however, another group of employees within executive agencies whose work is also essential to their successful operation. The role and perspective of this group, here described as administrators, is shaped by the organization in which they function, not by any craft or skill in which they specialize. Within public bureaucracy there are two particularly vital tasks that such administrators perform. The first is that of attending to certain auxiliary functions that are indispensable to the operation of any organization, such as the handling of funds and the maintenance of physical plant and equipment. The second, and more prominent, role is that of coordinating the work of professionals within the organization and establishing effective liaison with the community. These latter tasks have pushed administrators into positions of executive leadership in a good many organizations.

Policy as it develops within executive agencies — and within the government itself — is heavily influenced by pulling and hauling between professional and administrative points of view. Professionals are primarily committed to the attainment of the goals that their skill is designed to achieve. Administrators, if their function is that of providing staff services, are likely to emphasize economy in the use of resources. This is, for example, the common perspective of budget officers and purchasing officials. In a dichotomy of this sort, the concern of professionals is with the effectiveness of policy — the achievement of objectives no matter what the cost. Fiscal administrators, on the other hand, are principally concerned with efficiency in the use of the organization's assets — attaining results with a minimum expenditure of scarce resources upon which there are multiple claims within the organization.[8]

Administrators with more general responsibilities in executive or public relations capacities are likely to be far more sensitive than professionals to the need for compromise in pursuing objectives — the necessity of settling for half-a-loaf, or of taking the views of other groups and organizations into account in reaching decisions. Such administrators are a force for moderation in the policy process. The qualities needed in this kind of administrative role are a gift for negotiation and diplomacy, which stands in rather stark contrast to the fanatical zeal with which professionals frequently advocate their distinctive point of view.

In looking at the development of policy within administrative agencies, it is clear that a great deal of the energy and innovative force in the policy process comes from professionals. True enough, the perspective of professionals is often narrow. They commonly have difficulty in seeing a problem in its full breadth and complexity from the confines of their own specialty. Moreover, the inability of professionals to take costs into adequate account in the pursuit of policy goals, or to follow lines of authority and orderly procedure, is often a source of confusion and conflict within organizations.

But in the end it is professionals who are at the growing edge of policy. It is their skills that give agencies their problem-solving capacities; and their specialty often gives them foresight into the shape of things to come. Returning to the religious analogy, professionals frequently play the role of prophet in the policy process — seeing beforehand problems that lie far ahead. Scientists in such fields as nuclear energy, weapons development, and space exploration have been able to perform precisely this kind of prophetic function in recent years in the development of national science and defense policy.

The importance of their own role often leads professionals to disparage the contribution that administrators can make to an executive agency. From the professional's perspective, the administrator is often looked upon as merely a bookkeeper or, that ultimate insult, a "paper-shuffler." The professional commonly regards administrative rules and procedures that are designed to promote organizational efficiency as stifling to both energy and imagination. Generally, professionals believe that organizations should be subject only to loose and flexible supervision, rather than to the tight rein of control that administrators characteristically prefer.

> Irritation over the approval of travel is typical of the administrative "tight rein" against which professionals often rebel. They complain that such controls consume time they should be spending on professional work. One regarded the review of scientific positions (required by the personnel

officer) as "a waste of time." . . . Still another professional complained of the requirement that he make out officer fitness reports. "[I] do not regard this type of report as relevant to the functions of a scientific research organization." [9]

The stereotyped image of the professional in the eye of the administrator may be no less unflattering. Administrators in many agencies tend to look upon their role as primarily that of formulating policy with a realism and breadth of perspective that professionals by themselves could never provide. While these two contrasting outlooks engender tension and often conflict within executive agencies, both professionals and administrators have a vital and complementary role to play in the development of policy. If professionals provide such useful ingredients as imagination and technical skill, administrators can help insure that policy attains maximum results with the resources available, and that it is sensitive to the needs and interests of the community groups that will be affected by it.

This latter consideration is particularly important, since professional groups habitually frame programs in areas for which they are responsible in ways that may be more advantageous to themselves than to the groups affected by these policies. Administrators in city hospitals can represent patients or their families in the development of policies governing medical care, and at state universities administrators can play a similar role in seeing that courses and schedules are designed with the interests of the student as well as the professor in mind.

Of course, there are also situations in which administrators develop an excessive attachment to formal rules and procedural regularity in ways that are highly disadvantageous to clients — as, for example, the hospital administrator who insists upon patients being properly checked in and their financial status determined before they are treated. In a context of this sort, clients may turn to professionals and obtain sympathy and help in breaking through organizational red-tape.

The split between professionals and administrators has been examined here primarily as it operates between groups playing different roles within executive agencies. However, this cleavage in viewpoint can also characterize the relations between agencies. In the national government, for example, agencies that employ a high percentage of professional employees, such as the National Science Foundation, the National Aeronautics and Space Administration, and the National Institutes of Health, have a highly professional outlook that can generate sharp disagreement with an agency like the General Services Administration, which is, by way of contrast, thoroughly administrative in its orientation.

Of course, disparity in viewpoint between two professionalized agencies is equally possible. It is in fact such disagreement that provides the raison d'être for one of the most important roles that administrators play — the mediation of conflict between professional groups. Even in the United States, resources are not unlimited and priorities have to be established. Since all professional groups would regard the needs of their own area of concern as having first claim in any allocation decision, the role of the administrator in helping to determine the order in which needs will be met is a strategic source of influence over public policy. It is perhaps the greatest paradox of the policy-making process within bureaucracy that professionals, who have such great influence when program objectives are being determined, have so much less power over the allocation of the fiscal resources that enable objectives to be realized.

One current trend that is bound to have a very substantial impact on the future role of professionals in organizations is their increasing tendency to divide in a very partisan way on policy issues. This tendency has been the source of acrimony and even disruption at meetings of professional societies like the American Association for the Advancement of Science, as dissidents demand that their professional association take a strong stand on such issues as population control, the safety of nuclear reactors, or air and water pollution standards. One dimension of this dissent is the growing support among younger professionals for "whistle-blowing" — calling public attention to decisions and actions of a government agency for which they are working that they regard as not in the public interest, even though this activity may bring charges of disloyalty or even more severe sanctions from the agency and perhaps the professional association to which they belong.

Among many professional groups a cleavage is also emerging today between "hard-liners" and "soft-liners." This is not unlike the distinction so often drawn during American involvement in the Vietnam War between "hawks" and "doves" — the hawks favoring a tough military posture as an appropriate posture for the United

States in dealing with the North Vietnamese, and the doves being more favorably disposed toward a policy of negotiation and accommodation. On many other issues of public policy one can discern a similar kind of division among professionals. For example, there are ecologists who favor very strict measures to protect the environment while others are willing to modify standards of environmental control in order to achieve other policy goals — such as the development of energy resources. Likewise in the field of law enforcement, there are hawks who favor a very tough stand in dealing with criminals, while doves in the same professional area emphasize the importance of ameliorating social and economic conditions such as unemployment out of which crime emerges.

Bureaucracy: Insiders and Outsiders. In the United States today, it is possible for many individuals with a high standing in, for example, one of the scientific professions, for example, to participate directly in the process of policy-making within executive agencies without committing themselves to full-time government employment. This is evident especially, but not exclusively, in the case of university scientists who can retain positions in academic life while having a voice in the development of policy within the inner councils of public bureaucracy.

Commonly, the outsider gains this entree by serving in an advisory capacity to a government agency. The National Science Foundation and other professional agencies reach into private life to fill the membership of innumerable committees that help make governmental decisions on fellowships, grants for the support of scientific research, and the location of new laboratories or other facilities. In many cases, the scientists thus serving as advisers have considerably greater eminence in their own professions than scientists who are full-time government employees. As a result, these outside scientists tend to be deferred to on policy questions by their professional colleagues in the executive agencies in which they are jointly associated.

Outsiders holding advisory positions within bureaucracy have been at the center of some of the most celebrated policy disputes that have arisen within the national government since World War II. The struggle over the question of whether the United States should attempt to develop a hydrogen bomb had its focus in the General Advisory Committee to the Atomic Energy Commission —

a committee made up of distinguished scientists from outside the government. No single event did more to trigger discussion and re-appraisal of national security policy in the United States in the 1950s than the report of the so-called Gaither Committee, a presidential study group drawn from business and other institutions outside the government.[10] Thus, the American system of government "has developed its public service in such a way as to avoid creating a closed bureaucracy." A variety of groups are given an opportunity "to help determine public policy and to assist in its execution through an elaborate system of advisory machinery." [11]

Several factors help to account for the expanding role of outsiders in the internal deliberations of executive agencies. To some extent, it is a product of necessity. In many of the more highly skilled fields, public agencies cannot recruit enough high caliber personnel for full-time employment to meet their needs. The outsider, whether serving as adviser, consultant, or on temporary assignment with the agency, helps fill the gap created by this employment problem. Many talented outsiders will serve executive agencies on a temporary or ad hoc basis who could never be attracted to full-time government employment.

Moreover, the role of the outsider is such that he can contribute to the policy-making process certain qualities it would otherwise lack. Having a secure position in an institution other than the agency itself, he can speak his mind without editing his thoughts for fear of reprisal by his administrative superiors in government. This independence of judgment helps promote diversity of opinion within a bureaucratic environment in which the pressures toward conformity may otherwise be very strong. A president or the head of an executive department may also bring in outsiders to protect himself against domination by the strong vested interests and institutional ideologies of the agencies he normally supervises. In this context, the outsider can play the role of devil's advocate — speaking for points of view that would not ordinarily enter the discussion were it not for his presence. There is, of course, no certain guarantee that outsiders will always exhibit such independence of judgment. The money or prestige that outsiders accrue from their consulting role may be very important to them, and they may hesitate to take positions that are too strongly critical of the agency from which they derive these benefits.

But at the very least these newcomers will not have been so

thoroughly indoctrinated in the agency's institutional point of view as to be incapable of looking at problems in any but the traditional way. A chief disadvantage of the practice of confining policy positions to members of the career staff is commonly believed to be the fact that they have spent their working lives in the service of the agency and their attitudes have been entirely shaped and limited by its norms and experiences.

To be sure, this lateral entrance procedure may entail substantial costs. For one thing, any freshness of viewpoint that an outsider brings to an agency will almost certainly be accompanied by a lack of actual experience in dealing on a day-to-day basis with the problems that are its central concern. Originality may thus have to be purchased at some cost in terms of practical judgment. While a long-time agency administrator may be "in-bred" in his perspective, and have lost his zest for innovation, he may also have a keen eye for pitfalls that should be avoided in launching a new program.

In addition, the practice of allowing outsiders to make a lateral entrance into high-level positions without having served time in the ranks has a negative impact upon the morale of permanent employees who have spent their entire careers in the service of the agency and who see themselves being excluded from the most responsible jobs in the organization. In the long run lateral entrance can thus make it substantially more difficult to attract imaginative and capable personnel to permanent positions within the agency and in this way may actually reinforce mediocrity in the career staff. Some observers would cite the State Department as an example of an organization in which this development took place.

From an agency's perspective, there is also a measure of irresponsibility attached to an adviser's position, since the outsider does not have to put a policy into effect in an often hostile environment, or live with the consequences of a decision once it has been made. Many advisers may, in addition, have private attachments or interests that color the advice they give the agency. The Dixon-Yates controversy, for example, whose tremors shook American politics throughout most of the 1950s, had its origin in the fact that an adviser to the Bureau of the Budget was in a position to benefit personally from the recommendations he made to the government.[12]

"Conflict of interest" of this sort remains an enduring problem in the use of outside advisers or consultants by executive agencies. The possibility that these outsiders may benefit personally from their privileged influence over decision-making through membership on advisory committees has led to the enactment of a number of statutes designed to regulate this role, as, for example, the Federal Advisory Committee Act of 1972 requiring that the meetings of some 1,400 committees advising national agencies be open to the public.[13]

From the outsider's point of view, there are also liabilities attached to his position. While he can give advice, he has no real authority to see that this advice is taken. As an adviser or consultant, the outsider may find that trying to get an agency to follow his suggestions is a good deal like trying to push a box car uphill. It is this consideration that finally leads some outsiders to accept temporary government service in one of the agencies that provide employment opportunities through which outside professionals can exert influence at high levels of bureaucratic decision-making.

An executive agency as well as an individual may find it difficult to exercise real influence when the authority for putting policy decisions into effect rests in other hands. Consequently, an agency that has primarily advisory power may be forced to establish effective liaison with operating agencies in order to prevent its advice from being stillborn. The Council of Economic Advisers, for example, while established primarily to provide the president with competent advice on how best to preserve the health of the domestic economy, has also found it necessary to establish close and continuing relations with a number of executive agencies that wield important powers affecting economic stability. Chief among these agencies are the Bureau of the Budget, the Federal Reserve Board, and the Department of the Treasury. Ultimately, the impact of the council upon fiscal policy depends upon its ability to exercise influence over these organizations as well as over the president.

The practice of involving outsiders in the internal deliberations of executive agencies is a long-standing tradition in American bureaucracy. Its openness to outside penetration is in fact one of the distinctive characteristics of bureaucracy in the United States. As discussed earlier, this is most often seen as the problem of capture of a government agency by outside interests. But it also presents the danger of co-optation by the government of individuals who might otherwise be the most informed critics of official policy. Taking a potential critic into camp in this way may thus be regarded as an adroit technique through which the Department of

State, for example, can muffle public debate in controversial areas of foreign policy. This is another illustration of Harold Lasswell's "restriction by partial incorporation," [14] buying off potential critics by giving them a place in court.

But the custom of bringing outsiders into government is more than a method by which officials may draw the teeth of their opposition. It is also a means of infusing official policy with the values and attitudes of the community, or at least informed segments of it. More than that, it is an avenue through which the long-term critical capacities of the community may actually be expanded rather than contracted. Sooner or later, many outsiders who are drawn into the policy-making councils of bureaucracy leave government employment. When they do, the inside knowledge they have gained as a result of their government service enables them to become the most effective of all critics of official decisions. No one subjected the government's Vietnam policy to more searching or influential criticism than former officials of the Kennedy and Johnson administration. The criticisms of an outsider have much more credibility with the public if they come from a person who had once been an insider.

This is not, of course, to deny the possibility that such bureaucratic migrants may also become apologists for, rather than critics of, official doctrine. Sometimes they may only appear to speak from an independent position as private citizens, since in point of fact they are drawing pay as consultants or advisers from the agency whose politics they are defending. At best, however, the public dialogue as well as the bureaucratic may be greatly improved by having outsiders participate in the internal deliberations of executive agencies. The bureaucratic dialogue may immediately become more spirited, and the public dialogue eventually may become better informed.

Albert O. Hirschman has presented a stimulating analysis of the way in which the ability of members of organizations to leave or "exit" from their positions affects their capacity for independent thought on issues confronting the organization.[15] According to Hirschman, the possibility of such exit allows individuals to be much more vigorous in their criticism of errors in the organization's established policies. Organizations are thus much less likely to become moribund when their membership includes individuals who can exercise this exit option. This is the core of the case that can be made for having outsiders as well as insiders play an important role in organizational decision-making. By threatening to leave, or by actually doing so, outsiders can help alert organizations to problems that threaten their survival or vitality but that they might otherwise choose to ignore.

But the effectiveness of exit as a means of forcing an organization to reconsider the wisdom of its policies depends ultimately on the willingness of those leaving to make the reasons for their departure known. Here it should be noted that unlike other democratic countries such as Great Britain, the United States has no tradition of resignation over disagreements on policy among executive officials. The costs of exile from the Court appear to be too heavy for most outsiders in this country to bear.

> To quit the club! Be outside looking in!
> This outsideness, this unfamiliar land,
> From which few travellers ever get back in . . .
> I fear to break, I'll work within for change.[16]

Thus, there were no high-level resignations during the Johnson administration in protest over the Vietnam War, in spite of the fact that many of those who left government service during this period were later to proclaim that they had in fact opposed the war. But silent exit clearly has no impact in terms of reforming either policies or organizations.

Career Orientations. Not all the differences in outlook among the participants in bureaucratic policy-making spring from differences in the role that individuals play in organizations. If this were the case we would be able to predict bureaucratic behavior entirely from the axiom that "where one stands, depends on where one sits." We know, however, that role is not always a reliable predictor of policy outlook. During the latter stages of the Johnson administration, for example, Secretary of State Dean Rusk emerged as the principal spokesman for military solutions to the conflict in Vietnam, while Secretary of Defense Robert MacNamara became increasingly skeptical of its value.[17]

So there has been growing interest in the use of psychological variables to explain behavioral differences among participants in bureaucratic decision-making. This has led to the construction of a number of typologies that seek differences in bureaucratic outlook in terms of variations in career orientations that are related to differences in psychological predispositions. Anthony Downs, for example, presents a five-fold classification of bureaucrats as climbers, conservers, zealots, advocates, or statesmen, and each category has a distinctive set of motivations or behavioral patterns associated with it.[18]

Both climbers and conservers are motivated by self-interest. They see organizations as arenas in which they can achieve their personal goals. Climbers seek either advancement or an increase in the perquisites attached to their present job. They have a predilection for jumping from one bureau to another in order to improve their income or status. Conservers, on the other hand, are primarily concerned with holding on to what they already have. They seek not to advance themselves, but to avoid changes that might jeopardize their security. According to Downs, "the vast majority of officials . . . become conservers in the long-run," because their expectations of improving their position eventually erode after long service in the bureaucracy.[19]

The other three categories of officials in Downs' classification scheme are at least partially motivated by a concern for the public interest. One group of officials, whom Downs labels zealots, dedicate themselves to the pursuit of a particular policy goal that they regard as essential to the national welfare. They are imbued with a sense of mission. Another group equates the public interest with the preservation of the agency for which they work. These are called advocates and their identification is with an organization rather than a cause. Finally a group called statesmen takes a very broad and comprehensive view of all the factors and values that the public interest might seem to encompass. In Downs' view, statesmen "closely resemble the theoretical bureaucrats of public administration textbooks," [20] but their altruistic perspective does not fit well with the ambitious desires of most bureaus for expansion.

The Downs paradigm of career orientations is by no means the first of its kind. At a much earlier date Dwaine Marvick set out a system based on a cleavage between "institutionalists" and "specialists" that parallels the distinction drawn earlier between administrators and professionals.[21] He also includes a third "hybrid" type of bureaucrat whose characteristics and motivations are, as the term suggests, a mixture of those associated with the two other categories. Robert Presthus classifies career orientations in terms of the categories of upward-mobile, indifferent, and ambivalent — based essentially on variations in the degree of commitment that individuals have to the achievement of success in an organizational milieu.[22] The Marvick classification is notable for the fact that it is based on interviews conducted with federal employees, and is thus least subject to the charge of being "armchair" psychology, while the outstanding characteristic of the Presthus analysis is that it links career orientations very closely to differences in specific psychological characteristics.

It is in any event clear that while a public agency seeks to mold behavior in ways that are functional for it, the energy and effectiveness that any organization actually exhibits is very much affected by characteristics that the people it attracts already have. An organization that needs zeal and dedication for the achievement of its mission is not likely to reach its goal unless it is successful in recruiting personnel with a zealous temperament to its ranks. Moreover, the development of organizations may also be linked to changes in the temperament of the people working for them. The familiar tendency of reform agencies to lose their initial enthusiasm as they mature may be best explained by reference to the fact that their own employees are becoming more conservative with age.

CHARACTERISTICS OF THE POLICY SYSTEM

In many ways policy-making within executive agencies is indistinguishable from the process that takes place within legislative assemblies. Agencies respond to group pressures by modifying existing policies or by developing new ones. Bargaining or the adjustment of conflicting interests is as constant a feature of administrative politics as it is of the relations among legislators and legislative committees. Changes in policy tend to be — in Charles E. Lindblom's phrase — "incremental" in character.[23] Bureaucrats, like legislators, are wary of sweeping innovations that may disturb existing programs.

But while policy-making within bureaucracy bears many similarities to the style of decision-making within legislatures, there are differences also. To some extent these are differences in degree rather than kind, but they are nonetheless far from unimportant — as the discussion that follows will attempt to show. Three characteristics of bureaucratic policy-making are particularly significant in this regard: (1) the fact that authority in executive agencies is hierarchically structured; (2) the strong influence of professional or technical as distinct from political criteria in arriving at decisions; (3) the fact that the policy process is considerably less public in bureaucracy than it is in the legislature.

Hierarchy and Decision-Making. One of the most prominent characteristics of bureaucracy as a form of social organization is the distribution of authority in terms of hierarchical rank. In a bureaucratic setting officials at higher echelons normally expect to receive obedience from their subordinates. Hence, while policy deliberations in the legislature take place among elected officials who are equal in power in the salient respect that they all have but one vote on the questions that come before them, the policy dialogue in bureaucracy takes place among officials who are unequal in rank and consequent authority over final decision.

In recent times there has been a strong tendency in some of the more sophisticated appraisals of American public administration to discount the importance of hierarchy in bureaucracy. Emphasis has been placed instead on the extent to which subordinate officials can in fact determine policy outcomes — often in defiance of the views held by the heads of their own executive department. In the past, this weakness of hierarchy in American administration has commonly been explained in terms of political factors. Subordinate units are able to organize such strong constituency support that their hierarchical superiors are reduced to mere figureheads. Witness, for example, the following description of his own managerial impotence by a former director of the U.S. Employment Service:

> I started as director with a naive idea that I ran it, but I discovered that there was a part of the service that no director ran. This was the Veterans Employment Division, which did not even receive its mail in our mailroom. It had a special post office box downtown. When I tried to do something about the division, I learned that it took orders mainly from the Employment Committee of the American Legion. From then on I discussed the work of the division regularly with a committee of the American Legion in Indianapolis.[24]

One agency long famous for the degree of autonomy it has enjoyed within the executive apparatus is the Federal Bureau of Investigation. This attitude of independence from hierarchical control was given vivid expression by one FBI agent — responding angrily to the suggestion that his bureau follow the same policies in disclosing information as those practiced by the department in which the FBI is located:

> Don't tell me about the Justice Department. I don't care how they handle things. They do things their way, and we do things our way. They don't tell us how to handle our affairs, and we don't tell them. And another thing, when you have any questions about our work, don't call the Justice Department! Call us! We handle our own policy, not them. They don't tell us what to do! [25]

Another major factor helping to undermine hierarchical authority in administrative decision-making in recent years is the growing power of skilled professions in the work of public bureaucracy. "Especially is the hierarchical procedure weakened," Herbert A. Simon, Donald W. Smithburg, and Victor Thompson note, "as the social division of labor turns more and more people into indispensable and recondite specialists." [26] Professionalism is rapidly succeeding politics as the principal source of decentralization of authority in American bureaucracy. A subordinate who is a master of esoteric skills is no easier to dominate than one backed by a strongly entrenched group of political supporters.

Even in the face of these obstacles, however, hierarchy has become increasingly important in the operations of national bureaucracy in the United States as in other societies. The growing scope and complexity of bureaucratic activities engenders an irresistible need for coordination of effort that can only be achieved by vesting authority over decision-making in the higher ranks of bureaucracy. Left to themselves, subordinate units cannot escape duplication of effort or the pursuit of contradictory objectives. [27]

Moreover, the location of decision-making power at higher echelons makes it possible to achieve a more efficient allocation of resources among subordinate units. Certain activities can be centralized to conserve manpower, expenditures can be subject to more rigorous scrutiny by overhead agencies, and priorities can be estab-

lished to insure that resources are directed toward the more important goals of the organization. Considerations of economy thus
favor an increase in hierarchical authority, a factor of no small
importance in view of the mounting scale of public expenditures.

The doctrine of party government also supports an aggrandize-
ment of hierarchical influence in bureaucracy. A political party
that has won an election can only control the reins of government
if it can name its own partisans to the commanding heights of
bureaucracy where they can oversee and direct the activities of the
permanent and professional employees of government. Victor
Thompson has written a searching critique of the practice of sub-
ordinating skilled specialists to the commands of hierarchical
superiors who do not have equal technical competence.[28] However,
the objectives of a democratic society often require such subordination. Civilian control of the military, for example, can only be
achieved if military professionals are subject to hierarchical control
by civilian officials who, while having less knowledge of military
matters, are also less insulated from the preferences of the electorate.

Moreover, most proposals for reform in American politics reveal
great faith in the benefits that will come from an increase in hierarchy. Studies of Congress or of American political parties generally
stress the need to bolster the leadership role within such institutions. A traditional remedy for the ills of metropolitan life is to
replace the present multiplicity of governmental units with a single
authority having jurisdiction over all or a major part of the public
functions being performed in the region. Executive reform usually
centers on the idea of transferring power in a hierarchical direction
— by moving authority upwards from the bureaus to the departments or by strengthening the capacity of the White House to
monitor decisions being made within subordinate executive
agencies.

The presence of hierarchy as a dominant characteristic of
bureaucracy has varied consequences for the policy process. For one
thing, it enhances the likelihood that discrete policy decisions will
be consistent with each other. Hierarchy is thus an instrument for
coherent policy-making, and in this sense at least, an aid to rational
calculation in governmental decisions.[29] Activities that cannot be
geared together by a more or less self-regulating system of mutual
adjustment can be consciously coordinated. Moreover, under a

hierarchical system there is much less likelihood that the policy process will be stalemated. The exercise of hierarchical authority can break the log-jams created by conflict between two irreconcilable and equally powerful points of view at lower levels of decision. The growth of hierarchy thus reduces the necessity of relying upon interminable process of bargaining to arrive at policy decisions.

However, not all the consequences of hierarchy contribute to rational calculation in policy deliberations. The inequality of power inherent in hierarchy means that the views of highly placed individuals carry immense weight, not because of the persuasiveness of their arguments but simply because of the exalted status from which they speak. Subordinates may have to go along with policy decisions reached at higher levels even when they know that their superiors are wrong. Or they may find that their own advice, however well-founded, tends to be discounted because of their low standing in the hierarchy. The rationality of policy under a hierarchical system is thus constantly threatened by the disjunction between power and knowledge.

Ways of dealing with this problem do of course exist, but they are more in the nature of palliatives than antidotes. As noted earlier, subordinates can go over the head of their superior and betray their doubts regarding the wisdom of his judgment to other highly placed persons.[30] This is a course of action not without risk, and it is, therefore, open only to the venturesome. An advisory group made up of individuals having independent status outside the agency can also serve as a check upon folly in high places. But the difficulty here is that, as Dahl and Lindblom point out, men at the top of a hierarchy "decide when, in what conditions, and with whom consultation takes place." [31] Hierarchical superiors, from the president on down, have a penchant for selecting as advisers men who will give them the advice they want to hear.[32]

Hierarchy can thus be an immensely important factor inhibiting discussion and the free exchange of ideas in bureaucratic policy deliberations. In the past, it has been less a problem in American than in other bureaucratic systems. Reflecting as it does the general character of the political culture of which it is a part, bureaucracy in the United States has been characterized traditionally by pluralism rather than hierarchy in its organizational design. Whatever disadvantages this system may have had, it presented small possibility that debate might be stifled by deference to the views of a superior. The growth of hierarchy thus presents a continuing challenge to develop ways of dealing with the repressive effects it may have upon the policy dialogue.

The Professionalization of Policy. As has been noted earlier, bureaucracy is a governmental habitat in which expertise finds a wealth of opportunities to assert itself and to influence policy. Don K. Price once wrote that "the development of public policy and the methods of its administration owed less in the long run to the processes of conflict among political parties and social or economic pressure groups than to the more objective processes of research and discussion among professional groups." [33] This is the sense in which bureaucracy contributes to the impact of expertise upon policy decisions. It provides a setting in which experts in and out of government can get together to work on policy problems. Sometimes this occurs long before these problems become legislative issues or matters of public debate. In national security policy, for example, controversies over the feasibility of a hydrogen bomb, the need for greater expenditures on civil defense, and the wisdom of constructing an anti-missile system, were issues in bureaucracy long before they became matters of general public concern.

This is not, however, to suggest that political considerations are unimportant in bureaucratic deliberations. Nothing could be further from the truth. Executive agencies are part of the political system and their activities inevitably reflect the values and interests of outside groups. Certainly an agency's calculations as to the views of its constituency play a major role in the positions it takes on policy questions. It is rare to find an agricultural agency, for example, coming up with policy recommendations that are highly disadvantageous to the groups it serves merely because its own impartial analysis leads it to certain inevitable and irresistible professional conclusions.[34]

An executive agency, in addition, has certain power interests of its own to take into account in its evaluation of policy questions, and, as the history of the department of labor clearly reveals, these interests do not necessarily coincide with those of its constituency. During the 1930s, when labor legislation was taking giant steps forward under the impetus of the New Deal, the scope of the Department of Labor's administrative authority at first remained stationary, and then gradually even began to decline. While the department was suffering this setback, the trade union movement, upon which it chiefly depended for political support, was achieving a marked advance in both membership and power.

Hence an agency's participation in the policy process is bound to reflect its own distinct power interests quite apart from the needs of its constituency. Questions involving administrative jurisdiction, or the allocation of appropriations among different programs, will inevitably touch an agency's sensibilities upon its own organizational stature. No agency can be expected to preside enthusiastically over its own liquidation, and its perspectives on policy are bound to be shaped to some degree at least by considerations of its own organizational self-interest.

It is also important to guard against the fallacy — so dear to the heart of the American reform tradition — that a policy issue can be depoliticized by turning it over to bureaucracy. It is clear that most policy issues have a zero-sum quality — gains by some groups will have to be offset by losses for others. The decisions of bureaucrats, no less than those of politicians, will involve a redistribution of costs and benefits, and will as an inevitable result be political in nature. Moving authority for decision from politicians to bureaucrats means only that decisions will be made by different people and will result in a different allocation of resources among conflicting groups.

At the same time, however, it is equally vital to avoid the opposite fallacy of assuming that all policy-making in bureaucracy is entirely politicized — that technical and professional considerations have no weight whatsoever except perhaps as window-dressing. The truth of the matter is that a great many policy judgments hinge on technical advice that only professional personnel can supply. A health agency, for example, cannot make policy decisions or recommendations with respect to the smoking of cigarettes as a health problem until it has obtained the best scientific advice available on the relationship between smoking and a variety of illnesses now linked with the use of tobacco.

Likewise, a president, involved in the critical choices he has to make in the area of national security policy, will want to have the best advice he can get — whether from scientific or military sources — on the technical feasibility of certain courses of action. If a president chooses to ignore professional opinion altogether, the political consequences in terms of his own interests can be highly disadvantageous if not disastrous. Consequently, from the point of view of self-preservation alone, politicians are obliged to lean heavily upon the advice of bureaucratic experts in making policy decisions.

The importance of preserving the independence and integrity of certain kinds of expertise in government is thus very great. Traditionally, public agencies performing educational functions, like state universities, or at the national level governmental organizations engaged in a research function, like the Bureau of Labor Statistics or the Bureau of Standards, have been granted — by law or custom — a great deal of administrative autonomy. This freedom has been justified on the practical grounds that the performance of such functions as education and research demands an atmosphere completely free from political pressure.

But as more and more agencies play a policy-making role that requires reliance upon expert or at least nonpolitical standards, the need for professional autonomy begins to assert itself in all phases of bureaucratic policy-making. If policy decisions are to be effective, they must be informed by honest technical advice. This candor can only be secured if professionals are protected from reprisal for policy findings or recommendations that may be offensive to politically potent groups.

In some cases, an executive agency may choose to isolate a unit within its own organization from outside pressures, or even visibility, and charge it with making recommendations on politically sensitive issues. In this way an agency can at least be certain that nonpolitical criteria are taken into account in making policy decisions, even though political constraints may prevent decisions from being made on the basis of these criteria alone. This was the strategy followed by the Office of Price Administration during World War II, when it set up a Gasoline Eligibility Committee within its own organization to make recommendations to policy-making officials in terms of objective factors on the highly inflammable issue of allocating gasoline among domestic consumers.[35] With such a unit, an agency has some assurance that its policy deliberations are not being completely politicized.

In view of the roles that both political and nonpolitical criteria play in the bureaucratic policy process, the framing of public policy in a bureaucratic setting can be seen to involve a constant interplay between two quite different sets of factors. It becomes in effect a mixed system of politics and professionalism. Clearly political considerations have to be taken into account in bureaucratic policymaking in terms of the impact of decisions upon the outside community. At the same time, however, policy decisions certainly cannot fly in the face of professional advice when there is agreement among the experts as to the technically sound course of action.

The way in which political and administrative criteria interact in executive agencies can be seen in a decision made to close four field offices of the Department of Commerce. The forty-six field offices maintained by the department were first ranked in terms of the number of requests for information they received each month. The secretary of commerce then proceeded to select four offices for elimination from the fourteen that ranked lowest on this quantitative scale. While purely administrative criteria had determined which fourteen offices would be considered for elimination, political considerations were prominent in deciding which four out of the fourteen would actually be abolished.[36]

Under the system followed in the Department of Commerce field service case and in similar situations, a decision must not clearly flout professional or nonpolitical criteria. Other considerations can enter the decision-making process only when a decision is defensible on technical grounds. An agency head would leave himself highly vulnerable to criticism if he made decisions that were altogether indefensible in terms of professional standards. At the same time, any objective criteria used would ordinarily allow an executive to take other factors into account as well. An executive's options are not usually foreclosed by the findings of professionals within his organization.

The need to free executives from control by their professional staff in the framing of policy is certainly clear. In many areas of policy it is impossible to develop quantitative criteria as a basis for decision. Judgments must be made on the basis of incomplete evidence or on the basis of qualitative factors for which there is no evidence whatsoever. To be sure, this sometimes permits decisions to be affected by political considerations of a crude kind. At worst, administrative decisions may even be used to reward friends and punish enemies.

At the same time, however, restraints on the influence of professionals also make possible decisions that take into account a much broader range of considerations than are always encompassed within the perspective of a particular professional group in bureaucracy. Military officials, for example, may not see the diplomatic implications of a course of action they are recommending. Or doctors considering the location of a new city hospital may not give adequate weight to the needs and interests of the prospective patients who will use this medical facility.[37] It is thus possible to see and to find examples of "politics" as corrupting the process of professional decision in bureaucracy. It is also possible to see it as greatly expanding the horizons of bureaucratic decision-makers and enabling policy to satisfy the needs of much wider segments of the public.

Secrecy and Public Policy. The policy process as it is carried on within legislatures is by no means entirely public in character. In the national government, for example, a great many legislative committee meetings at which vital policy decisions are reached are held in secret. For example, the conference committee meetings at which differences between House and Senate bills are hammered out, were long held in secret, or, in less invidious terms, conducted in private.[38] Many hearings involving national security matters are also conducted in secret, though this is often because executive officials themselves ask that the meetings be closed to the public.

At the same time, however, the legislature is primarily a public institution. The public, if not always the private, activities of its members are open to constant scrutiny from the outside world. Its debates are conducted in public. The investigations and interrogations of its committees, if not visible on a day-to-day basis, are eventually printed in exhaustive detail as a public record. Whatever disadvantages the legislative policy-making process may exhibit, it has a striking asset — the fact that its deliberations and concerns are so easily known to those who will be affected by them. Citizens thus have an opportunity to make their views known on pending legislative issues before final decisions are made.

The bureaucratic policy process is, by way of contrast, a quite invisible part of government. The environment of bureaucracy is a cloistered sanctuary as compared with the limelight of publicity in which a legislative assembly normally operates. Though an executive agency may hold public hearings, or conduct press conferences, or release news bulletins of one kind or another, it controls, to a far greater extent than does the legislature, the information available to the public on its internal deliberations and decisions. The meetings, conferences, negotiations, and agreements through which bureaucratic policy decisions are reached can only be dimly seen through the opaque exterior that an administrative agency presents to the outside world. In some areas of administrative activity information is made available only through "leaks," interviews with "informed" sources, or an unexpected disclosure of secrets that were meant to be kept by a departing member of the inner circle. Bureaucracy did not invent secrecy in American government. The Founding Fathers, for example, found it expedient to conduct the deliberations of the Constitutional Convention at Philadelphia in 1787 in private long before there was an administrative establishment of any consequence in the United States. But the growth of bureaucracy in American government has certainly brought about an enormous expansion in the secretiveness with which public policy is made.

As noted earlier, there are important respects in which this secrecy contributes to the effectiveness of governmental decisions. At least in the early stages of policy development, a good many proposals benefit from private discussions. It is possible, for example, to explore certain courses of action in private that could much less easily be discussed in public, such as the use of the American government's funds to disseminate information on birth control at home or abroad. Except for a few hardy individuals, "thinking about the unthinkable" — in Herman Kahn's revealing phrase — as an enterprise much more easily conducted in private than in public.

Since privacy is conducive to candor in policy deliberations, administrative policy-making may permit a more honest exploration of alternatives than is possible in the legislature. Men are less often compelled to edit out of their discussions "dangerous thoughts" that might get them into trouble if they were widely known. Such privacy would be an unqualified benefit to rational calculation in policy deliberations were it not for the fact, previously noted, that it also serves to constrict the number of alternatives considered by excluding many informed individuals from the discussion process.[39]

But it is true that the greater degree of privacy characteristic of bureaucratic operations does promote accommodation and compromise in the development of public policy. Participants in administrative discussions can back down more easily on positions they have previously taken if they have not put their earlier point of view on public record. Compromise solutions that may be difficult to explain to constituents can be more easily agreed to in private than in public, since the responsibility for decision is in this case obscure. Since stalemate would be a worse alternative for the groups whose interests are involved, privacy may have a constructive effect upon the policy process by encouraging such mutual adjustment of interests.

Even though there are advantageous aspects of privacy in policy deliberations, the fact remains that the costs of this characteristic of bureaucratic policy-making are also high. Many executive officials make decisions on policy questions without having full access to the facts in possession of the government that are relevant to these decisions because of the restrictions of secrecy. When policies are determined in private, the sources of influence on these decisions may be unknown, and many groups whose interests are affected may not be consulted at all.[40]

Finally, it is much more difficult to identify and reverse mistakes when policy deliberations and decisions are made in secret by some chosen few — the saints rather than the sinners. This is a particular problem in foreign affairs where the possibility of irreversible error — of a fait accompli that cannot be undone — is heightened by the fact that so much of policy formulation takes place in the cloistered corridors of bureaucracy. In domestic policy, on the other hand, there is such a constant process of interaction among executive agencies, legislative committees, and community groups that very little of what is decided can be long concealed. It is hard to escape the conclusion that the more widely a policy proposal is discussed, the more likely it is that whatever defects it has will be exposed.

Congress has made innumerable efforts to limit the amount of secrecy in which executive agencies engage, including periodic investigations and the passage of laws attempting to establish the public's right to obtain information from the executive branch. But even this reform legislation has permitted the withholding of information in certain specified situations — as, for example, when legitimate claims to privacy on the part of citizens might be endangered by the release of data in the government's files. These so-called "exemptions" from the principle of disclosure have often been seized upon by administrative agencies to justify secrecy. Consider, for example, this description of the way in which the Freedom of Information Act was administered after its first enactment in 1966:

> The bureaucracy did not want this law . . . this attitude of opposition has manifested itself during the first years of the act's operation in excessive processing fees, response delays, and pleas of ignorance when petitioned for documents in terms other than the exact title or other type of precise identification.[41]

Congressional opponents of executive secrecy saw the way in which the 1966 law was being administered as a clear case of bureaucratic sabotage of legislative intent. Consequently, the Freedom of Information Act was greatly strengthened in 1974 and reenacted in 1975 after President Ford's veto.

One striking paradox emerges from any discussion of policy-making as it is carried on within a bureaucratic setting. This is the fact that Weber and other early students of the subject saw bureaucracy as the ultimate triumph of rationality while many critics see it today as having characteristics that contribute instead to irrationality in decision. As indicated in earlier discussion, bureaucratic organizations provide societies with a capacity to handle problems and to provide services that are indispensable for the functioning of a civilized society in a modern industrialized environment. Yet, as we have also seen, bureaucratic organizations are closely associated in the eyes of many people today with irrationality — with having characteristics including a hierarchical distribution of authority and a penchant for secrecy that seriously handicap their ability to arrive at sensible decisions on issues of public policy.

The tension between these varying perspectives on bureaucracy has been constant in the modern consciousness. Societies have sought to reap the benefits of using large complex organizations for a variety of purposes, but they have retained a deep suspicion that these organizations block the achievement of many social goals and contribute to the dehumanization of society by their insistence upon the primacy of form over substance. In short, as Martin Albrow has noted: "Two incompatible concepts — bureaucracy as administrative efficiency and bureaucracy as administrative inefficiency — compete for space in twentieth-century theory."[42]

Notes

1. H. H. Gerth and C. Wright Mills, *From Max Weber: Essays in Sociology* (New York: Oxford University Press, 1946), p. 234.
2 John Stuart Mill, *On Liberty* (New York: Appleton-Century-Crofts, 1947), p. 115.
3. For a full account of the factors and forces underlying this rebellion, see Gary Hershey, *Protest in the Public Service* (Lexington, Mass.: Lexington Books, D.C. Heath and Co., 1973).
4 See Charles E. Lindblom, *The Intelligence of Democracy* (New York: The Free Press, 1965). A study of the attitudes of career officials toward political appointees showed that these appointees are generally held in high esteem. See M. Kent Jennings, Milton C. Cummings, Jr., and Franklin P. Kilpatrick, "Trusted Leaders: Perceptions of Appointed Federal Officials," *Public Opinion Quarterly* 30 (Fall 1966): 368–84.
5. However, as noted earlier, an agency executive often has to tread a tightrope in wooing his subordinates without alienating important constituency groups. In contemporary urban politics, for example, a police commissioner faces the difficult task of handling the "police brutality" issue to satisfy both the members of his own department and civil rights organizations in the city.
6. For a thorough and absorbing account of some vital chapters in the New York experience, see Gerald Benjamin, *Race Relations and the New York City Commission on Human Rights* (Ithaca, N.Y.: Cornell University Press, 1974).
7. For an illuminating discussion of the role of the professional in organizations, see Amitai Etzioni, "Authority Structure and Organizational Effectiveness," *Administrative Science Quarterly* 4 (June 1959): 43–67. An analysis of the attitudes and behavior of professionals in more specifically governmental organizations may be found in John J. Corson and R. Shale Paul, *Men Near the Top* (Baltimore: The Johns Hopkins Press, 1966), pp. 77–102.
8. Cf. the distinction between efficiency and effectiveness in Amitai Etzioni, *Modern Organizations* (Englewood Cliffs, N.J.: Prentice-Hall, 1964), pp. 8–10. Herbert Simon, *Administrative Behavior* (New York: Macmillan, 2nd ed., 1957), presents a similar contrast between "efficiency" and "adequacy."
9. Corson and Paul, *Men Near the Top*, pp. 90–91. The best study of professionals and their role in government is Corinne L. Gilb, *Hidden Hierarchics* (New York: Harper and Row, 1966).
10. See Morton H. Halperin, "The Gaither Committee and the Policy Process," *World Politics* 13 (April 1961): 360–84. The list of committee members is given on pp. 361–62, footnotes 5 and 6.
11. Don K. Price, *Government and Science* (New York: New York University Press, 1954), p. 200. See also the discussion of "in-and-outers" in Richard E. Neustadt, "White House and Whitehall," *The Public Interest*, no. 2 (Winter 1966): 59–61.

12. See Aaron Wildavsky, *Dixon-Yates: A Study in Power Politics* (New Haven: Yale University Press, 1962).

13. See Mark V. Nadel, "Corporate Secrecy and Political Accountability," *Public Administration Review* 35 (January/February 1975): 16.

14. See Harold Lasswell, *Politics: Who Gets What, When, How* (New York: Whittlesey, 1936), p. 166.

15. Albert O. Hirschman, *Exit, Voice, and Loyalty* (Cambridge: Harvard University Press, 1970).

16. Barbara Garson, *MacBird!*, as quoted in Hirschman, *Exit*, p. 115.

17. See David Halberstam, *The Best and the Brightest* (New York: Random House, 1972), for one of the best accounts we have of the role of personality in shaping decisions at high levels of executive policy-making.

18. Anthony Downs, *Inside Bureaucracy* (Boston: Little, Brown, 1967).

19. Ibid., p. 99.

20. Ibid., p. 89

21. Dwaine Marvick, *Career Perspectives in a Bureaucratic Setting* (Ann Arbor: University of Michigan Press, 1954).

22. Robert Presthus, *The Organizational Society* (New York: Alfred A. Knopf, 1962).

23. "Incremental" decision-making is a central theme in David Braybrooke and Charles E. Lindblom, *A Strategy of Decision* (New York: Free Press of Glencoe, 1963).

24. Marver Bernstein, *The Job of the Federal Executive* (Washington, D.C.: The Brookings Institution, 1958).

25. Allen Weinstein, "Opening the FBI Files: An Interim Report," *Smith Alumnae Quarterly* LXVI (February 1975): 14. I am indebted to Lynne Brown for calling this reference to my attention.

26. Herbert A. Simon, Donald W. Smithburg, and Victor Thompson, *Public Administration* (New York: Alfred A. Knopf, 1950), p. 200. There is a perceptive discussion of the impact of hierarchy upon decision-making in Harold L. Wilensky, *Organizational Intelligence* (New York: Basic Books, 1967), pp. 42–48.

27. Cf. also, on this point, the discussion on p. 144.

28. Victor A. Thompson, *Modern Organization* (New York: Alfred A. Knopf, 1961).

29. For an analysis of the advantages of hierarchy as a form of social organization, see Robert A. Dahl and Charles E. Lindblom, *Politics, Economics, and Welfare* (New York: Harper & Bros., 1953), pp. 236–43.

30. See p. 112.

31. Dahl and Lindblom, *Politics, Economics, and Welfare*, p. 227.

32. See the earlier discussion of this point on pp. 19–20.

33. Price, *Government and Science*, p. v. See also the discussion of the "professional state" in Frederick C. Mosher, *Democracy and the Public Service* (New York: Oxford University Press, 1968), pp. 99–133.

34. For an interesting account of the troubles that beset one agricultural agency when it pursued research to conclusions that were disadvantageous to a group that considered itself part of the agency's constituency, see Charles M. Hardin, "The Bureau of Agricultural Economics Under Fire: A Study in Valuation Conflicts," *Journal of Farm Economics* XXVIII (August 1946): 635–68.

35. Harold Stein, ed., *Public Administration and Policy Development* (New York: Harcourt Brace, 1952), pp. 749–59.

36. See Kathryn Smul Arnow, "The Department of Commerce Field Service,"

The Inter-University Case Program (University, Ala.: University of Alabama Press, 1954).

37. Decisions on the location of facilities such as schools and hospitals often generate such conflicts between professional and community groups. See, for example, Edward Banfield, *Political Influence* (New York: The Free Press of Glencoe, 1961), pp. 15–56, 159–89.

38. As a result of pressures from Common Cause and other public interest organizations, as well as the growth of reform sentiment within Congress itself, there has been a marked decline in the number of committee meetings conducted in secret.

39. See p. 6.

40. An analysis of the impact of administrative secrecy upon policy decisions may be found in Wilensky, *Organizational Intelligence*, esp. pp. 66–74.

41. Harold C. Relyea, "Opening Government to Public Scrutiny: A Decade of Federal Efforts," *Public Administration Review* 35 (January/February 1975): 4. Of course, a great deal of administrative secrecy is designed to serve the interests of outside groups rather than bureaucrats themselves. See Francis E. Rourke, "Bureaucratic Secrecy and Its Constituents," *The Bureaucrat* 1 (Summer 1972): 116–21.

42. Martin Albrow, *Bureaucracy* (New York: Praeger, 1970), p. 31. See also Eugene P. Dvorin and Robert H. Simmons, *From Amoral to Humane Bureaucracy* (San Francisco: The Canfield Press, 1972).

CHAPTER SIX

New Designs for Policy-Making

As was indicated in earlier discussions, the design of the system through which executive agencies participate in policy-making has been structured by two not always consistent objectives — responsiveness and effectiveness. Bureaucrats are expected to serve the needs of the public — as the public reveals its needs — and to use the most effective means available for achieving the goals defined for their organization.

Today as in the past, continuing efforts are being made to enhance the likelihood that bureaucratic decisions and behavior will meet these standards of responsiveness and effectiveness. Administrative reform has been a high priority objective in the United States since the 1930s, when the executive apparatus began its ascent to power in modern American politics. In this chapter we will look at three of the main areas in which these reform efforts have been concentrated — administrative reorganization, the quantification of decision-making, and the amelioration of pathologies to which all large organizational structures seem inevitably to be subject.

Reform and Reorganization

Much of the history of administrative reform in the United States has centered on the search for a style of organization that would broaden the perspective of executive agencies.[1] As public administration was shaped by the forces ascendant in nineteenth and early twentieth century politics, it seemed to many reformers that policy decisions tended to reflect too narrow a set of interests. Authority for designing programs was widely dispersed among subordinate units of the executive branch, and their decisions responded not to the needs of broad segments of the public, but more commonly to the pressures of small clientele groups that held individual bureaus in captivity.

Beginning in the 1930s, it thus became a primary objective of administrative reform to reshape the structure of the executive branch so that power could be centered, not at the lower and presumably more parochial echelons of bureaucracy, but in the hands of departmental executives where it was expected that the interests of wider segments of the public would be taken into account in making policy choices. The location of decision-making power in subordinate agencies and bureaus was thus identified in the traditional reform theory of administrative organization with a limited perspective in policy-making, while the transfer of power to top-level executives was looked upon as a method by which the horizons of policy could be greatly broadened.

The effort to achieve an executive-centered system of administrative organization was vigorously pursued at all levels of government in the United States. However, as is usually the case in matters of administration, the national government took the lead in organizational reform. The report of the President's Committee on Administrative Management in 1937, as well as the findings and recommendations of two Hoover Commissions in 1949 and 1955, led the way toward a very substantial expansion in executive authority in national administration in the United States. This administrative reorganization had a variety of objectives, including the saving of money by eliminating duplication of effort, and the grouping of related activities into cohesive units. But at the heart of the traditional reorganization movement was the belief that policy-making could be more far-sighted and comprehensive in outlook when responsibility for decision rested with higher rather than lower authority.

The movement toward a more hierarchical system of organization was part of the long-standing quest in the United States for administrative arrangements that would enable agencies to promote the "public interest" in their decision-making processes. To be sure, there has not always been agreement in the literature of public administration on the meaning of so elusive a concept as the public interest. Some have seen it as signifying no more than the sum of the private interests affected by particular administrative decisions, while others have regarded it as embodying collective interests that transcend the needs of particular groups in the community. But there would certainly be widespread agreement with the proposition that this public interest standard requires administrative agencies to take the needs of broader as well as narrower publics into account in designing their policies and procedures.[2]

However, even as the reorganization movement was largely successful in centralizing authority for decision-making in the hands of departmental executives, voices were increasingly heard suggesting that the old-fashioned system of dispersed authority in administrative organization was not altogether without value for public administration. What might be called a revisionist critique thus began to emerge at the very moment when the traditional reorganization movement had largely won the day and become the "conventional wisdom" on questions of organization design.

Revisionists pointed out, for example, that a structural pattern under which administrative authority is widely dispersed has the advantage of promoting a variety of points of view and a more spirited dialogue among executive agencies in the development of policy. In an analysis of President Franklin D. Roosevelt's style as an administrator, Arthur M. Schlesinger, Jr. argues that the secret of Roosevelt's success was his ability to keep administrative authority scattered so as to generate disputes among his subordinates that would broaden his own options while preventing any one adviser from gaining excessive influence over him. Roosevelt, writes Schlesinger, "deliberately organized — or disorganized — his system of command to insure that important decisions were passed on to the top. His favorite technique was to keep grants of authority incomplete, jurisdictions uncertain, charters overlapping." [3] It should be noted, however, that if Roosevelt derived advantages from a system of decentralized administrative authority, he also, as president, did a great deal to further administrative centralization, through, for example, the appointment of the President's Committee on Administrative Management, and the steps he subsequently took to carry out its centralizing recommendations.

The fact that dispersion in administrative authority enlivens the process of discussion within bureaucracy is not the only ground on which it can be defended. The argument can also be made that such fragmentation helps to link authority with knowledge, insofar as the professional personnel in subordinate bureaus and agencies commonly know more about the technical aspects of the policy issues with which they are dealing than do departmental executives. Form this perspective, the traditional reform effort to shift authority from bureaus up to departments can be looked upon as aggravating the split between knowledge and power that is endemic in modern bureaucracy.[4] Under a system of centralized authority, subordinates inevitably find themselves being overruled by superiors whose professional competence is far less than their own. While these upper-echelon officials may have a broader perspective on the problems under consideration, they lack the depth of knowledge on particular issues that their subordinates possess.

Moreover, it is not always certain that officials who are more highly placed in bureaucracy will actually have a clearer view of the public interest in administrative decision-making than their subordinates. Aaron Wildavsky, for one, argues to the contrary:

> . . . the partial-view-of-the-public interest approach is preferable to the total-view-of-the-public interest approach, which is so often urged as being superior. . . . The danger of omitting important values is much greater when participants neglect the values in their immediate care in favor of what seems to them a broader view. . . . A partial adversary system in which the various interests compete for control of policy (under agreed-upon rules) seems more likely to result in reasonable decisions — that is, decisions that take account of the multiplicity of values involved — than one in which the best policy is assumed to be discoverable by a well-intentioned search for the public interest for all by everyone.[5]

Wildavsky's argument here parallels very closely the defense by Charles E. Lindblom of fragmented as opposed to comprehensive approaches to policy development: "different points of view taken by the different groups in government serve to make each group something of a watchdog for certain variables against others." [6]

But while such voices of dissent have been heard with increasing frequency, the fact remains that official studies and reports at all levels of government still recommend an increase in hierarchy as the standard way of improving the organizational design of the executive branch. Limitations on administrative centralization today more often rest on practical than on theoretical considerations. Subordinate agencies represent important repositories of specialized skills, and as long as knowledge is widely distributed at lower levels of the hierarchy, power must in large measure follow suit.

Of course, it is not inevitable that a choice be made in designing a policy system between an arrangement that allows for the articulation of specialized and intense interests, and one that reflects the needs of broader and less self-interested publics. The fact of the matter is that it is possible to incorporate both perspectives in making decisions in any area of policy. In public higher education in the states, for example, the individual colleges and universities have been left with substantial autonomy to promote their own goals, while at the same time it has become increasingly common to establish a coordinating agency or "super-board" to look at higher education from the perspective of the needs and problems of the entire state. In this way, both Wildavsky's "partial-view-of-the-public interest" and a "total-view-of-the-public interest" may simultaneously inform and guide policy development. Incremental and comprehensive ways of looking at policy issues need not always be mutually exclusive.

An alternative to conventional reorganization strategy that has gained much prominence in recent years is the proposal to decentralize authority in executive agencies, and to allow those for whom services are being provided to participate in decisions in which they have a stake. This proposal has been put forward with particular vigor in the case of services designed for low-income groups in cities, perhaps because the gulf between the street-level bureaucrats who furnish these services and their impoverished urban clientele is both wide and visible.[7]

A decentralized administrative structure in which the citizens being served have a voice in decision-making has particular appeal in the case of agencies that are trying to effect some basic transformation in their clients, rather than simply providing them with a service for which they have a need. In the case of agencies dealing with an impoverished clientele, for example, it can be argued that the poor will increase their own sense of personal efficacy if they participate in administrative decisions affecting them. Such participation may thus help overcome the demoralization and dependence that often accompany economic deprivation and perhaps enable a poverty agency to restore some of its clients to an independent and productive role in society.

In addition to cases where such clientele transformation is a real possibility, there is also strong justification for citizen involvement in agency decision-making when the side-effects, or what economists call the "externalities" of decisions, are particularly acute, and when an agency is dominated by a professional group that may not always be sensitive to these side-effects. Consider, for example, the case of a planning department in a state or locality, whose designs for a new highway may have grievous, but unanticipated, consequences for some of the areas through which the agency's traffic engineers have routed it.

The technique of allowing the members of affected groups to become involved in policy decisions is far from a new departure in American administration. Farmers have long been granted the right to participate in deciding many questions in agricultural policy either by direct vote, or by representation in advisory groups that have a dominant role in policy decisions. Techniques of representing the public in the process of policy development were also prominent in the operation of the Selective Service System in the United States, as well as in the system of grazing administration carried on by the Bureau of Land Management in the West.

It is not always self-evident, however, what form citizen involvement in policy-making should take even where it does seem to be appropriate. In some areas of policy citizen groups have been granted a virtual veto power over policies affecting their interests. This has long been true in certain aspects of agricultural and conservation administration, and many supporters of antipoverty programs advocate a similar arrangement for programs affecting the urban poor. More common, however, is the practice followed by many planning departments of holding public hearings at which they present proposals for new highways or changes in land use, and citizens or neighborhood organizations may appear and offer objections to these projects. If these objections seem well-founded, or are backed by substantial community pressure, then the planning department may be forced to abandon or revise its initial proposals.

It should be noted that while the decentralization movement aims to make executive agencies more sensitive to the special needs of the particular groups they serve, a radically different orientation toward organizational reform is taken by public interest groups that seek instead to broaden the perspectives of regulatory agencies by making them less responsive to their immediate clientele and more sensitive to the needs of the public-at-large, whose interests as consumers of transportation, energy, and other goods and services are greatly affected by the decisions of these regulatory bodies. A major paradox of contemporary public administration is thus the fact that while some reformers are trying to make agencies more responsive to the specialized constituencies they serve, others are trying to make them less so.

Watergate perhaps did as much damage as any other event in modern times to the traditional devotion of reformers to a centralized executive structure. It demonstrated very clearly that decentralization of authority provides some measure of protection against the corrupt use of power at the top of the organization. In the Watergate episode, subordinate agencies with some tradition of autonomy, like the Federal Bureau of Investigation and the Internal Revenue Service, resisted White House efforts to involve them in illegal activity and became important sources of information on the misconduct of presidential aides for the press and eventually the Special Prosecutor's Office.

In light of Watergate, it is ironic to recall that three decades earlier the Brownlow Commission on executive reorganization had recommended to President Roosevelt that he create the first full-fledged White House staff to assist him in managing the executive branch. The primary attribute of this staff, the commission urged, should be a "passion for anonymity." Little could Brownlow and his colleagues have anticipated in 1937 that the passion for anonymity of one White House staff member would lead him in 1972 to procure dark glasses and a red wig to carry out his assigned tasks, which included breaking into the national headquarters of the Democratic party in the dead of night.

DATA AND DECISIONS

No objective in public administration in recent years has been more vigorously pursued than the attempt to make more effective use of quantitative data in making policy decisions. This trend toward quantification in decision-making partly reflects the fact that management techniques are now available such as operations research and systems analysis that greatly enhance the capacity of administrators to base their decisions upon more solid ground than speculation and hunch. Moreover, the vast sums of money now being expended by executive agencies create strong public pressures for greater economy. Since it promises to bring about a more efficient use of financial resources to achieve program goals, quantified decision-making thus has appeal for political officials as well as management specialists.

The changing technology of management that has given rise to the new vogue for quantification largely reflects innovations in software, in the sense of techniques such as cost-benefit analysis that make it possible to link data to decision more effectively. But it rests upon changes in management hardware as well, particularly the advent of data-processing equipment. Computers have the capacity to sort out large masses of information and to do so with a speed that enables data to be compiled soon enough to have an impact upon decision. To be sure, most of the employment of computers to date in public as well as in private administration has been in the routine areas of decision — helping administrators keep track of payrolls, clients, and other management records. The use of computers at more complex levels of policy decision is as yet very limited in its development, although simulation techniques are being used to test the impact of high-level decisions even before they are put into effect.[8]

At the heart of the effort to put policy decisions on a more rational basis have been reforms in the budgetary process, since the budget is in a sense the expression of policy in quantitative terms. Attempts were made as early as the 1930s to find better methods of relating the use of budgetary resources to the achievement of policy objectives.[9] These efforts reached something of a climax during the 1960s, when a comprehensive form of program budgeting called PPB, a planning-programming-budgeting system, was established in the national government. Under PPB, it was hoped, the costs of alternative ways of achieving policy objectives could be clearly identified, and resources concentrated on those programs best calculated to achieve objectives at the least cost.

The PPB system was initiated in the Department of Defense in 1961 in an effort to obtain a maximum return on the vast sums of money being expended to achieve national security objectives. It enjoyed at least the image of success in that area of policy, largely perhaps because the achievement of defense goals is so easily linked to the construction and procurement of weapons systems. Alternative ways of assuring the nation's security through armaments could be expressed in dollar figures and subjected to comparative evaluation on a quantitative basis. In 1965 the PPB system was extended by President Johnson to a wide variety of domestic programs as well. Thereafter, it began to languish, until it was finally replaced in the Nixon administration as an executive panacea by "management by objectives" — MBO — a technique designed to point executive agencies toward achieving their goals rather than comparing different ways of using their resources.[10]

The troubles PPB encountered are typical of the difficulties that confront all efforts to apply the magic of managerial science to public administration. Many programs proved stubbornly resistant to quantification. Foreign policy objectives, for example, cannot readily be converted into budgetary alternatives. Cost-benefit ratios are difficult to work out in an area in which the pursuit of program goals is not primarily a matter of spending money.[11] Similar difficulties confront efforts to apply quantitative methods to domestic programs. Hard facts on which measures of achievement can be based are not easy to come by. Who, for example, can calculate the ultimate benefits that may accrue to society from a federally financed program of educational enrichment designed for slum children in the elementary grades? The task of measuring the costs of a particular course of action can also be extraordinarily difficult, especially since it is usually necessary to bring nonmonetary costs within the sphere of calculation.

Moreover, no system of quantification now available permits comparisons of the relative pay-off of achieving disparate goals such as welfare, education, or public health. The hard choices of policy, allocating scarce resources among widely different programs, still remain essentially political in character. No set of quantitative techniques can transform policy-making into a purely managerial process. Whether it is more important to use resources to achieve foreign policy objectives, or to spend them on one or more of a variety of domestic programs are questions that defy analysis in purely quantitative terms.

At the same time, however, the fact that quantification does have such limitations provides reassurance for those who fear that the advent of some new managerial technology will strip power from

the public and its elected representatives and shift it to a techno-
cratic elite skilled in operations research, systems analysis, and the
use of the new computer hardware. From this perspective it is com-
forting to know that politics plays a central role even in a com-
puterized policy process. Major policy decisions invariably involve
a choice between conflicting values — the relative importance of, for
example, rehabilitating slum areas as opposed to a highway construction program. The larger decisions of a society thus remain
inextricably a matter of public preference. Indeed, it can be argued
that the rise of technologies that improve our ability to make
choices makes us more aware of choices that can be made and thus
increases the public role in decision-making.[12]

Moreover, with or without managerial science, pressures from
community groups, or the calculations of politicians regarding the
opinion of these groups, will always represent salient factors in
making policy choices in a democratic society. While a particular
program may rank very low on the scale of cost-benefit ratios, if it
enjoys extensive public support, or if the president or a sufficient
number of congressmen calculate that it has broad public appeal,
then its adverse standing in terms of economic rationality is not likely
to be a fatal defect. Now as in the past, policy responds to the
balance of forces within the community, or the perceptions of politicians regarding this balance, as well as to the analytical data generated by quantitative systems of management. Hence, political
considerations, in the sense of both value conflicts and the play of
conflicting forces within the community, continue to have a major
influence upon administrative decisions even in a setting of managerial science.

From the point of view of an executive agency itself, it is often
imperative to follow a strategy of organizational opportunism in
the pursuit of its goals, no matter what priorities strict adherence
to cost-benefit data might seem to require. A program for which a
great deal of community support exists at a particular point in time
may have to be vigorously pursued even though costs are high and
benefits relatively low, in order that the opportunity created by an
immediately favorable climate of opinion may not be missed. The
advent of managerial science does not abolish the need for adroit
administrative statecraft.

At its best, any quantitative technique of management serves as
an important instrument of clarification in the design and develop-

ment of an executive agency's program. While it may not always provide answers in making policy choices, it certainly centers attention on the important questions and provides a framework within which the pursuit of many objectives can be most intelligently carried on. As one observer put it: "What the new intellectual techniques, such as those used in PPBS, attempt to provide are methods by which those who make the decisions about how the government should direct its efforts can increase their awareness of the conditions and consequences of their choices and can clarify the elements that, explicitly or implicitly, enter into their judgments." [13] Certainly, it is clear that a great many agencies have very little information about how well they are doing on the mission on which they are embarked.

Again, however, political realities must be taken into account. Investigations conducted in the 1960s by Congress and the press disclosed that the Subversive Activities Control Board was accomplishing very little in the way of achieving its statutory objective of identifying and deterring subversive activity. However, in spite of this evidence of its ineffectiveness, the agency continued to command strong support in Congress and elsewhere. As the work of Murray Edelman brings out, an agency can have enormously important symbolic value for its adherents quite apart from its tangible accomplishments.[14] In the case of the Subversive Activities Control Board, the symbol of opposition to communism that it represented far outweighed in the eyes of its supporters the fact that it was not doing anything. The agency was abolished only in 1973 when changes in the political climate finally made it politically safe for Congress and the president to withdraw financial support and thus liquidate it.

The greatest danger that techniques of managerial science present is the possibility that they may arm error with the seeming support of scientifically established fact, in this way giving ill-advised policies greater credence than they would otherwise have. When this occurs, the finely honed rationalizing instruments of managerial science can become dispensers of irrationality measured out with mathematical precision.[15] During the Vietnam War, for example, managerial specialists were constantly inventing and using measures of American success in the effort to suppress the Viet Cong and pacify the countryside — such as the ill-famed "body count." These measures had great influence with policy-makers, even though they proved in the end only to be instruments of self-deception.

One situation in which quantitative data may have extraordinary weight is where most of the considerations involved in decision-making have intangible dimensions. Here numerical measurements may command a great deal of deference simply because they are precise quantities in a sea of uncertainty. To preserve rationality in decision, it is essential therefore, that the use of data be hedged about with a sense of the limitations as well as the possibilities of such factual information. A balanced perspective of this kind can be most confidently expected when sophistication in the use of quantitative techniques of analysis is widely distributed throughout the government, so that weak arguments in a policy discussion do not gain an unwarranted advantage merely because they are put in the language of managerial science.

Overcoming Bureaucratic Pathologies

Among the many ways in which the American experience with bureaucracy differs from the European, none is more striking than the fact that executive agencies in the United States have so often been looked upon as major instruments of change in social and economic policy, while in Europe bureaucracy has historically been regarded as a chief source of institutional support for the status quo. Indeed, it is no exaggeration to say that public bureaucracy has been a revolutionary force in American society insofar as it has provided a channel through which submerged groups could assert their power. Farmers in the last century and more recently trade unionists and the urban poor have looked to executive agencies for the redress of their grievances against more powerful segments of society, and the services of these organizations have provided the means by which the welfare and status of these disadvantaged groups have been greatly improved. In Europe, on the other hand, such groups more commonly have identified bureaucracy as part of the political system that must be overcome if public policy is to be changed in ways that are advantageous for them.

In the 1930s, for example, public bureaucracy was a principal instrument through which the New Deal revolutionized American society. Agencies such as the Securities and Exchange Commission, the Social Security Board, and the National Labor Relations Board quickly became identified as major institutions through which the power of the mighty could be put down, and the welfare of the humble exalted. Certainly it was in this light that these agencies were regarded by business groups hostile to the New Deal. From the point of view of American conservatives, bureaucracy was both the symbol and the source of radical change in American society in the 1930s. Fulminations against bureaucratic power dominated conservative rhetoric, while at the same time defense of the role of administrative agencies in government came to be a conditioned reflex for the American liberal.

More recently, however, a new reform perspective on the relationship between bureaucracy and change has begun to emerge. Increasingly, the established bureaucracies in welfare, education, foreign affairs, and a variety of other areas have come to be looked upon as obstacles to imaginative and creative thought in their own area of policy responsibility. Reformers interested in taking bold new steps in dealing with the problems of the "permanently poor," or raising the level of aspirations on the part of children in the slum schools, or in achieving some new breakthrough in international relations that would reduce the possibility of nuclear war have found that a frequent source of resistance to change in each of these areas is the executive agency chiefly responsible for policy development. Witness, for example, the following description of the role of public bureaucracy in New York City:

> The leaders of the city's bureaucracies are a conservative force in the political contest. The stakes they seek are primarily those that minimize innovation and change. Their drive for autonomy is largely an effort to reduce the influence of the outside "movers and shakers" upon settled routines. . . . The policy and procedural *status quo* of today, or perhaps yesterday's in some matters, is their accepted milieu. . . . In the city's political process the leaders of the organized bureaucracies are an anchor, not a force driving forward.[16]

No agency better exemplifies the shift in the reform perspective on bureaucracy than the Tennessee Valley Authority. When it was established in the 1930s, TVA was the supreme organizational expression of the liberal belief that a public agency could serve as an instrument of change. The agency was created to invigorate the economy and elevate the welfare of the entire valley region through comprehensive planning and control of the development of its water and other natural resources. Though bitterly opposed in its early years by private power companies and other conservative interests in the valley area, the agency eventually won a secure standing as a successful public agency, especially after World War II, when the less developed countries came to see it as a model for the way in which they might quickly industrialize themselves through governmental development of hydroelectric power resources.

By the 1970s, however, TVA was no longer a beacon light for change. In the eyes of reformers, it had transformed itself into one of the major vested interests in the valley region. Environmentalists were particularly incensed by the agency's support of strip-mining and other practices considered hazardous to the environment in its ever-expanding quest for new sources of energy. Ecology groups even took the agency into court in an effort to prevent it from constructing a dam that they alleged would do substantial damage to recreational use of adjacent land.

As the TVA experience so clearly reveals, bureaucracy today is as frequently a target of criticism from the left in politics as it is from the right. However, while the burden of complaint from conservatives is likely to be the charge that executive agencies are exceeding their authority, liberal groups more frequently complain that agencies are doing far less than their responsibility requires them to do. On one point, however, there is very often a convergence of viewpoint — the belief that bureaucrats are unimaginative, reluctant to accept new ideas, and extraordinarily slow to abandon policies that are clearly unsuccessful. In short, rigidity in outlook on matters of policy is a pathology increasingly attributed to bureaucracy by critics from all segments of the political spectrum.

The quickest and most thorough-going method of insuring a fresh approach in administration is to establish a new agency. When it is feasible, this alternative is the preferred choice of reformers, since it allows for the recruitment of an entirely new cadre of personnel, thus eliminating the necessity of converting old hands to new ideas. A new agency is also free from some of the constraints that limit the flexibility of established organizations, such as a long-standing association with certain pressure groups, or an arrangement of mutual accommodation with legislators upon whom an agency may depend for fiscal support. Moreover, such an agency has not yet acquired the administrative habits and experience that it may eventually come to regard as the sum total of human wisdom in its own area of policy. But it is certainly ironic that a major remedy for the ills of bureaucracy should be the creation of additional bureaucracies.

Similar in its effect to the creation of a new agency is a significant change in the jurisdiction or resources vested in an existing administrative organization. In the 1960s, for example, a flood of educational legislation greatly broadened the responsibilities of the U.S. Office of Education. This led to an influx of new personnel as well as to a reorganization of the agency, which altered not only its internal structure of power, but also the pattern of external influences to which the agency was subject from outside groups.[17] While not all observers would agree that such measures achieved a genuine improvement in the character of the Office of Education, this experience does point up the possibility of administrative renaissance — an old agency may be given a new lease on life through administrative reorganization, the influx of new personnel, or a dramatic shift in the scope of its activities.

Innovation in the development of policy can also be encouraged by the practice of having executive agencies contract with organizations outside of government to undertake studies and make proposals on policy issues. In recent decades there has been a proliferation of arrangements at all levels of government under which private organizations perform research at the request of public agencies for the guidance of policy-makers. Much of this kind of activity has been delegated to universities, but a new phenomenon has also emerged — the so-called "side-car" corporation, private organizations like the Rand Corporation or the Institute for Defense Analyses, which exist almost entirely on the revenue they receive from conducting studies for government agencies.

A number of advantages accrue from the use of outside organizations for research purposes. For one thing these organizations are free from the restrictions that surround government hiring procedures and can, as a result, often recruit a very high caliber of professional personnel. Since they have no vested interests to protect in arguing for one line of policy rather than another, the conclusions they arrive at are often regarded as a good deal more reliable than the findings of a research unit under the jurisdiction of a line agency. Within government itself, research is often used not so much to find answers to questions as to build support for solutions that policy-makers have already decided upon, or to advance the jurisdictional interests of a particular agency. Policy studies conducted by outside organizations are less susceptible to this tendency, though they are not immune to it. One study of RAND suggests that the findings contained in its reports are largely prestructured by their governmental sponsors.[18]

Outside organizations can be used not only for advisory or consultative purposes but also for the direct operation of governmentally supported activities. The atomic energy program, for example, as well as a wide variety of research and development projects sponsored by agencies like the National Institutes of Health and the National Aeronautics and Space Agency, are largely carried on through government contracts with outside organizations, particularly, though not exclusively, universities. The Office of Economic Opportunity administered the overwhelming majority of its antipoverty activities through private, nonprofit corporations called community action agencies. This system of what Don K. Price has called "federalism by contract"[19] is to a large extent motivated by the belief that nongovernmental organizations can be considerably more imaginative in their approach to policy problems and much more flexible in their day-to-day operations than public agencies.

Another bureaucratic pathology that has drawn widespread criticism is what is perceived to be administrative inertia — the failure of bureaucrats to deal vigorously and imaginatively with problems that are high on the agenda of public concern. In part this is simply a matter of bureaucrats choosing to ignore problems that lie within their official responsibility, since executive agencies have an enormous capacity for "nondecision."[20] They can see to it that issues do not arise in areas in which, to an outside observer, action may seem to be urgently needed. In part also, bureaucratic inertia manifests itself through the fact that executive agencies find difficulty in shifting their sights when past policies are no longer appropriate to present conditions.

This latter aspect of bureaucratic inertia — the difficulty administrative officials have in admitting and reversing mistakes — sharply contradicts one of the major justifications traditionally offered for transferring power over policy development from legislative assemblies to executive agencies. This was the expectation that administrative agencies would be considerably more flexible than legislatures in their response to changing environmental conditions — mainly because they were organizations continuously in existence, which could use the discretionary authority given them to adapt policy to emerging needs. In point of fact, however, public bureaucracies on frequent occasion have proved to be quite rigid in their policy commitments, unable to change courses of action with which they as institutions or the reputations of their leaders have become identified.

Sometimes the resistance of bureaucracy to new outlooks may be simply a function of the slowness of movement of large organizations — the fact that a broad and complex pattern of consensus must be developed before change can take place in vast organizational systems in which there are many centers of power and innumerable points at which decision can be blocked. However, it is also possible for organizations to acquire vested interests in policies that are, from the point of view of society at large, dysfunctional, and to resist change, not because it is difficult for them to move in response to new stimuli, but simply because they have acquired a stake in the policies they are already following. If existing programs serve the comfort and convenience of a public agency's employees, or conform to their own professional view of what should be done, then they may develop deeply entrenched resistance to any alteration in such policies.

Private organizations can, of course, exhibit this same tendency toward organizational inertia. However, by so doing, they run the risk that the public will cease to purchase, or otherwise support, the goods and services they supply, and a private organization's survival may be quickly threatened by its failure to adapt to the needs of the community it serves. Public agencies, on the other hand, perform vital functions that a community cannot do without, and they frequently hold a monopoly position in providing such services. Except in the case of agencies that enjoy only precarious political support, citizens cannot directly threaten the existence of a public agency as a means of forcing it to put their needs before those it may choose to set for itself.[21]

Discontent with bureaucracy in the modern state also centers on a feature of bureaucratic policy-making that has already been extensively discussed.[22] This is the hierarchical characteristic of executive agencies — the fact that superior officials have considerable power over the careers and hence the views of their subordinates. In this context, it is impossible to expect anything resembling a completely free discussion in which all alternatives are given equal consideration. Especially when they are involved in conflict situations with external groups, organizations will inevitably tend to emphasize solidarity rather than dissent as an institutional virtue. A decision-making system subject to constraints of this sort is incapable of meeting all the requirements of a democratic society committed — in theory at least — to full and frank exploration of all options as a prerequisite to rational decision. It is not unfair to say that more of the literature on policy failure focuses on the pathologies in bureaucratic communications brought on by hierarchy than on any other subject.

Some students of organizations now argue that hierarchy has outlived its usefulness and that organizations in the future will be structured more like teams of equals sharing responsibility for decision-making than pyramids of authority linked together by a chain of command. Warren Bennis is conspicuously identified with the view that "temporary" organizations will be the dominant bureaucratic model of the future — organizations put together to solve particular problems and then dissolved.[23] The impermanence of these organizations provides protection against the vices that arise when bureaucracies furnish people with lifetime careers and fixed interests that any change threatens to disturb.

But while such temporary organizations, or what Alvin Toffler calls "adhocracies,"[24] have been created in the public sector and have dealt effectively with many special or emergency problems, they tend in government at least to supplement rather than to supplant permanent agencies. Indeed, they are often staffed with career officials drawn from the regular executive apparatus and the behavior of these officials must be guided by the expectation that they will someday return to their bureaucratic home. As an alternative organizational form, adhocracies do not, therefore, seem likely to bring an end to either hierarchy or bureaucracy in government.

The most drastic of all cures available for the ills of bureaucracy is simply that of attempting to solve as few social problems as possible through the creation of large-scale organizations. The limitations of bureaucracy can thus be overcome by avoiding the use of bureaucracy.[25] Of course, there are many sectors of policy like foreign affairs and national defense where societies have no choice but to rely on the talents of their public organizations. And a similar dependence on organized officialdom exists in many areas on the domestic side of policy as well.

Competition is a remedy many see as a means of stimulating public organizations to higher levels of performance. Like monopolies in the private sector, it is argued, public agencies lack incentive to perform effectively because the consumers of their services have nowhere else to go to obtain a more satisfactory product. Hence, critics of the public schools argue for an educational voucher system, which would permit parents to choose among a variety of schools on which to spend their tax dollars. Such a system would encourage the development of alternative schools that would compete with one another for enrollment. It would thus subject public agencies to the discipline of the market. Schools that satisfied a public demand for the kind of education they provided would thrive; those that did not would suffer a loss of resources. This voucher system has not been used extensively enough to know how well it would work in the field of education, and it is difficult to see how it could be applied in many other areas of policy.[26]

But it is certainly clear that in the absence of market penalties for poor performance, public bureaucracies often seem to be most rewarded when they are not accomplishing their objectives and to be least rewarded, if not actually punished, when they are. A police department is much more likely to receive an increase in appropriation when there is a crime wave, much more likely to have its budget cut when the streets are comparatively serene. An internal study of the operation of New York City's public hospitals showed that the lion's share's of appropriations went to hospitals that were doing the poorest job in terms of eighteen performance criteria. Under this skewed incentive system, it can be argued that it pays a public agency not to do too well the thing it is charged with doing.

But in much of the discussion of bureaucratic pathology there has been a tendency to overlook the fact that the fault for policy failure may well lie elsewhere than in the organizations charged with responsibility for implementing policy goals. Sometimes policies fail because bureaucratic organizations are given ends to achieve — as was the case in the War on Poverty under President Johnson — for which we do not yet have the requisite means or the appropriate technologies. When agencies have elusive goals like what we called earlier "clientele transformation" in fields such as education and welfare, we enter areas where there are many more "experts" than there is demonstrable expertise. Bureaucratic organizations are bound to fail if they are given tasks that are beyond human competence at the point in time at which they are assigned.

In other cases policies may fail because the resources allocated for their achievement are insufficient to obtain successful results. A goal might be within a country's grasp, if it was prepared to spend the necessary resources, but it is unwilling to do so. In either of these situations — whether policy fails because of inadequate technology or insufficient resources — the fault may lie not with bureaucratic pathologies but with elected officials who promise more than they can deliver, or the public itself, which is unwilling to pay the costs necessary to attain some of its goals.

Notes

1. For a comprehensive look at the whole subject of administrative reform, see Gerald E. Caiden, *Administrative Reform* (Chicago: Aldine, 1969).
2. For a discussion of these early efforts to use the public interest as a touchstone in appraising administrative decision-making, see Pendleton Herring, *Public Administration and the Public Interest* (New York: McGraw-Hill, 1936), esp. pp. 377–99; Emmette S. Redford, *Ideal and Practice in Public Administration* (University, Ala.: University of Alabama Press, 1958), pp. 107–37; Glendon Schubert, *The Public Interest* (New York: Free Press of Glencoe, 1960), esp. pp. 64–74, 106–23, 173–86; and Frank J. Sorauf, "The Public Interest Reconsidered," *Journal of Politics* XIX (November 1957): 616–39.
3. Arthur M. Schlesinger, Jr., *The Coming of the New Deal* (Boston: Houghton Mifflin Co., 1959), pp. 527–28. Cf. also on this point the discussion in Richard E. Neustadt, *Presidential Power* (New York: John Wiley & Sons, 1960), pp. 156–58.
4. The best treatment of this problem is by Victor Thompson, *Modern Organization* (New York: Alfred A. Knopf, 1961).
5. Aaron Wildavsky, *The Politics of the Budgetary Process* (Boston: Little, Brown and Co., 2nd ed., 1974), pp. 166–67.
6. Charles E. Lindblom, "Policy Analysis," *American Economic Review* 48 (June 1958): 306. More distantly, Wildavsky's viewpoint corresponds to the concept of "piecemeal" social planning developed in the work of Karl Pop-

per, *The Open Society and Its Enemies* (New York: Harper & Row, Torchbook edition, 1963), esp. I: 157–68.

7. Perhaps the best study of the decentralization movement is by Alan A. Altshuler, *Community Control* (New York: Pegasus, 1970). For an analysis and bibliography on citizen participation techniques, see Robert K. Yin, William A. Lucas, Peter L. Szanton, and J. Andrew Spindler, *Citizen Organizations: Increasing Client Control over Services* (Santa Monica, Calif.: The Rand Corporation, 1973).

8. Some of the more advanced uses of computers in administrative decision-making are explored in Herbert Simon, *The New Science of Management Decision* (New York: Harper & Row, 1960). See also Martin Greenberger, ed., *Computers, Communications, and the Public Interest* (Baltimore: The Johns Hopkins Press, 1971).

9. The historical antecedents of PPB are traced in Allen Schick, "The Road to PPB," *Public Administration Review* XXVI (December 1966): 243–58. See also the letter by Frederick C. Mosher in the *Public Administration Review* XXVII (March 1967): 67–71.

10. For a review of the decline and fall of PPBS, see Allen Schick, "A Death in the Bureaucracy: The Demise of Federal PPB," *Public Administration Review* 33 (March/April 1973): 146–56.

11. See, in this regard, the initial memorandum of the Senate Subcommittee on National Security and International Operations, *Planning-Programming-Budgeting*, 90th Cong., 1st sess., committee print, August 11, 1967.

12. See Victor C. Ferkiss, *Technological Man* (New York: George Braziller, Inc., 1969), pp. 136–37. Cf. also Daniel Bell, *The Coming of Post-Industrial Society* (New York: Basic Books, 1973), pp. 341–67.

13. Virginia Held, "PPBS Comes to Washington," *The Public Interest*, no. 4 (Summer 1966): 114.

14. See Murray Edelman, *The Symbolic Uses of Politics* (Urbana, Ill.: University of Illinois Press, 1964), esp. pp. 44–72.

15. For some reservations regarding the role of PPB in national security policy-making, see Klaus Knorr, "On the Cost-Effectiveness Approach to Military Research and Development," *Bulletin of the Atomic Scientists* XXII (November 1966): 11–14.

16. Wallace S. Sayre and Herbert Kaufman, *Governing New York City* (New York: Russell Sage Foundation, 1960), p. 407. Other studies that point up the obstructive role of bureaucratic organizations in policy development include Gilbert Y. Steiner, *Social Insecurity: The Politics of Welfare* (Chicago, Ill.: Rand McNally & Co., 1966), and David Rogers, *110 Livingston Street* (New York: Random House, 1968).

17. See Stephen K. Bailey, "The Office of Education and the Education Act of 1965," *Inter-University Case Program, No. 100* (Indianapolis: Bobbs Merrill Co., 1966).

18. See Philip Green, "Science, Government and the Case of RAND: A Singular Pluralism," *World Politics* XX (January 1968): 301–26.

19. Don K. Price, *Government and Science* (New York: New York University Press, 1954), pp. 65–94.

20. This is a term introduced to guide the analysis of political power in urban communities by Peter Bachrach and Morton S. Baratz, *Power and Poverty* (New York: Oxford University Press, 1970). Matthew Crenson has used this concept with great skill in analyzing the development of air pollution policy in American cities. See *The Unpolitics of Air Pollution* (Baltimore: The Johns Hopkins Press, 1971).

21. For a systematic analysis of factors affecting innovation in public and private organizations, see James G. March and Herbert A. Simon, *Organizations* (New York: John Wiley & Sons, 1958), pp. 172–210.

22. See pp. 128–32.

23. Warren G. Bennis, *Changing Organizations* (New York: McGraw-Hill, 1966). Cf. also Frederick C. Thayer, *An End to Hierarchy! An End to Competition!* (New York: New Viewpoints, 1973).

24. Alvin Toffler, *Future Shock* (New York: Random House, 1970), pp. 112–35.

25. For some suggestive comments on this alternative, see James Q. Wilson, "The Bureaucracy Problem," *The Public Interest,* no. 6 (Winter 1967): 3–9.

26. The literature on "public choice" is the best exploration of the possibility of using market forces to control bureaucratic behavior. See Vincent Ostrom, *The Intellectual Crisis in American Public Administration* (University, Ala.: University of Alabama Press, 1971). Cf. also William A. Niskanen, *Bureaucracy and Representative Government* (Chicago: Aldine Atherton, 1971), and Gary L. Wamsley and Mayer N. Zald, *The Political Economy of Public Organizations* (Lexington, Mass.: Lexington Books, D.C. Heath and Co., 1973).

CHAPTER SEVEN

Bureaucracy as
a Power Elite

A specter that has haunted political life throughout this century is the possibility that bureaucrats will come to occupy so commanding a position in the policy process as to become in effect a power elite — dominating all government decisions in which they participate.[1] A growing reliance upon the skills of bureaucrats in the operation of modern government has thus been coupled with a pervasive distrust of bureaucratic power. On the part of conservatives this has been largely a fear of civilian bureaucrats taking over areas of social and economic decision that properly ought to be left in private hands. From the liberal side, fear of bureaucracy centers on the growing power of national security agencies — not only the military establishment but also such organizations as the Central Intelligence Agency and the Federal Bureau of Investigation in the United States.

Concern over bureaucratic power is closely akin to the fear of technology that has figured so large in contemporary political thought. Critics of technology are alarmed by the possibility that modern civilization will be dominated by the machines that have been its most conspicuous product. There is continuing apprehension that mankind will be transformed and ultimately dehumanized by intimate association with its own mechanical and electronic contrivances. A cinematic expression of this fear is the movie *2001*, which depicts a voyage to Jupiter in which the people manning the spacecraft are virtually robots and a computer emerges as the only one aboard capable of real feeling. But conforming to the traditional fear of technology, the computer eventually becomes the instrument of the crew's destruction.

From this perspective, bureaucracy is viewed as part of the technology of modern life — a way of organizing human efforts so that people can replicate the efficiency of the machine. Just as there is fear that the instruments men construct will go out of control — attacking and perhaps destroying their human creators — so there is apprehension that the organizations people devise to achieve their goals may eventually become their masters rather than their servants. The ancient Greeks attached the term *hubris* to the excessive pride men often take in their own capacity for invention and achievement. The widespread reaction against technology and bureaucracy in more recent times suggests that human beings can also be quite fearful that their creations may represent a threat to them.

Fear of bureaucracy has sometimes taken extravagant form in modern society, exaggerating beyond all bounds of possibility the capacity or likely intention of particular agencies to assume a controlling voice over governmental decisions. Paradoxically, this fear of bureaucracy often coexists with another attitude with which it is in sharp contradiction — the feeling noted in the previous chapter that bureaucrats are timid, unimaginative, and reluctant to make decisions. The stereotype of a bureaucracy that is boundless in its appetite for power may thus co-exist with an image of bureaucracy paralyzed with indecision when confronted with an opportunity to exercise authority.

It is clear in any case that even if bureaucrats had the inordinate appetite for power commonly attributed to them, their role in the governmental process is hedged about by a wide variety of constraints that limit their ability to exercise influence. These limitations arise partly from sources external to executive agencies, the fact that bureaucrats do not rule alone in any area of public policy. They rest also upon factors indigenous to bureaucracy itself — "inner checks" built into the structure of administrative organization and the behavior of bureaucrats. As noted earlier, for example many bureaucrats look upon power as a burden rather than an opportunity, and tend to shift it from their hands whenever possible.

However, if bureaucrats do not have a monopoly power over policy-making, it is clear that they play a strategic role in the process by which decisions are made. While they are unable to rule alone, no one in modern politics can rule without them. And when administrators cannot achieve their own goals, they may be able to prevent others from achieving goals to which they are opposed. It is as a "veto group," or perhaps through its ability to keep certain matters from coming to decision at all, that an executive agency may actually exercise its most formidable influence. This chapter examines both the pattern of constraints to which bureaucratic power is subject, and the extent to which executive agencies yet manage to play a leading role in the determination of public policy.

COMPETITION AMONG ELITES

A fundamental restriction under which bureaucrats operate is the fact that they share control over decisions with other elites in the political system. Whatever else it may be, theirs is not an exclusive power. One of the most important groups with which they compete for influence are the political elites in both the executive and legislative branches of government. In addition, the leaders of nongovernmental organizations with a continuing interest in the issues over which executive agencies have jurisdiction also exert strong influence on their decisions. In some areas of policy public agencies may be little more than pawns in the hands of the private groups with which they are associated. Less pervasive but nonetheless critical is the periodic participation by the courts and the media of communication in the processes of policy-making. Both of these institutions have long helped to define and set boundaries upon the power of bureaucrats.

The interaction of bureaucrats with each of these elite groups in the development of public policy will be examined in the section that follows. It should, however, be noted at the outset that bureaucratic influence is by no means a constant factor in the policy process. As pointed out earlier,[2] the bureaucrat may exert measurably more influence in one policy setting than he does in another, or the influence of a particular professional group may be much greater in one governmental jurisdiction than it is in an adjacent community. Significant variations in the balance of power between bureaucrats and other elites may also occur at different periods as a result of changes in the context in which policy is being made. "Power in America," David Riesman once wrote, is "situational and mercurial." [3] Clearly, this is no less true of bureaucratic than it is of other forms of influence.

Political Elites. The relationship between bureaucratic and political elites in the United States is enormously complicated by the fact that varied sets of political leaders simultaneously occupy positions of authority with respect to administrative agencies. On the one hand, there is a set of executive politicians with which agencies must share power — a chief executive such as the president, a governor, or a mayor, and his appointed or elected administrative subordinates. On the legislative side, there are, under a bicameral system of representation such as prevails in the United States, two or more groups of leaders who participate with bureaucrats in making policy decisions.

In general the presence of these varied political elites in the policy process helps to create a system of multiple constraints upon bureaucratic behavior and decision. Executive agencies in the national government operate within limits set by the president and his agents with respect to budgets, personnel, and policy, as well as restrictions imposed by Congress through statutes, appropriation acts, or the threat of investigation. In addition, agencies are subject to patterns of informal political pressure from both legislative and executive leaders because they are so heavily dependent upon these officials for fiscal and other resources necessary to sustain their programs.

Of course, by winning favor with one political elite, bureaucrats can limit the authority of another. Through the assiduous cultivation of support from key legislative groups, administrative agencies have been able to reduce, sometimes to the vanishing point, the controls exerted over them by executive politicians. An agency can also use one group of legislators as a shield against another.[4] The Pentagon can always rely on strong support from its congressional allies whenever it comes under criticism in the national legislature. Political elites compete with each other as well as with bureaucrats, and executive agencies often serve as valuable allies in the struggle for power among politicians. However, it is questionable if bureaucrats always increase their influence in the policy system by playing one political elite off against another. When, for example, they decrease the control exercised over them by executive politicians, they may so intensify the degree of their subordination to legislative elites that they become in effect "legislative agencies."

A much more promising strategy for any administrative agency is that of building up sources of outside support to which political leaders in both the executive and legislative branches of government will defer. The power of political leaders comes ultimately from the public. Having been elected to office, they, more than any other participants in the policy process, can be said to be most closely in tune with public opinion and to represent its sovereign authority in a democratic society. To the extent that bureaucrats speak for significant publics, they can expect some of the same deference from political leaders that these outside groups ordinarily receive. However it is filtered to them, public opinion is a formidable force in the calculations of both political and bureaucratic elites.

Traditionally, it has been assumed that bureaucrats derive their greatest advantage in their interaction with political elites from both their expertise in the technical areas of policy and their continuity in office. However, the fact of the matter is that, whatever may be true in other societies, these assets of expertise and continuity are not always the exclusive possession of the bureaucrat in the American political system. Legislative leaders in key committees may gain as expert a command of policy problems as any of the bureaucrats with whom they deal. In the United States, legislators tend to specialize in their policy interests — a tendency that is encouraged by the strong power vested in legislative committees. This specialization, along with the fact that many legislators enjoy long tenure in office, helps to offset the superior professional qualifications that bureaucrats ordinarily bring to policy deliberations.[5]

In short, it is, as noted before, incorrect to regard a political elite's influence as resting solely upon the power of numbers — upon the ability of the politician to reflect and generate public pressures, while bureaucratic influence is attributed entirely to the professional skills of administrators. Politicians, too, may in time acquire formidable credentials as experts, if they do not bring such credentials with them when they come to office. But if political officials share in the bureaucratic asset of expertise, bureaucrats themselves are not wholly without the ability to mobilize public support in behalf of their own policy positions. The competition between bureaucratic and political elites is thus one in which either side can bring to bear both political and professional resources.

Public and Private Power. The leaders of nongovernmental organizations also represent an elite with which bureaucrats must frequently share power. This is obvious in the case of nongovernmental organizations that have an adversary relationship with an executive agency. If a government agency administers laws that limit the discretion of, for example, business organizations, these outside organizations will in turn bend every effort to see to it that the powers of such a regulatory agency are confined within narrow limits.

What is not perhaps quite so obvious is the fact that the leaders of nongovernment organizations that are allies rather than antagonists of an executive agency may also represent a significant constraint upon the scope of its influence. But in international politics alliances often limit the options open to states that participate in such arrangements — preventing them from following certain courses of action and requiring them to fulfill commitments that they might well prefer to forget. In a similar fashion, the alliances forged by the Department of Agriculture, Commerce, and Labor with their farm, business, and trade union clientele, while of great value in enhancing the constituency strength of these agencies, nonetheless require that each department defer to the views of its nongovernmental allies in adopting policy positions. The development of political support through the negotiation of alliances with outside organizations is thus a means by which the power of executive agencies is circumscribed as well as extended.

In some areas of the economy the decisions of administrative agencies may have life or death consequences for the business firms under their jurisdiction. A television station requires a license from the FCC in order to operate, a utility cannot raise its rate without the permission of a public service commission, no drug company can market a new product without the approval of the Food and Drug Administration, and all large firms face the constant possibility of antitrust prosecution by the Justice Department.

But even in the case of relationships where such apparent administrative hegemony exists, the business firms subject to regulation have a great deal to say about the direction and development of policy within the agency under whose jurisdiction they lie. They can exert great influence on legislation affecting the scope of the agency's power, the fate of its requests for appropriations, or appointments of the executives who have ultimate control over the agency's decisions. In such patterns of reciprocal influence, the balance between public and private power in American society is not easy to discern.[6]

The Media and Bureaucracy. In some areas of policy, it is representatives of the media of communication who generate the most substantial outside constraint upon the decisions and activities of government officials. The news media have a powerful voice in the development of policy because they both reflect and have the ability to shape the contours of public opinion.[7] Nowhere is the influence of the media more keenly felt than in the agencies dealing with foreign policy, since only the media have the capacity to gather and disseminate information that may challenge the viewpoint of government officials on areas remote from the average citizen's power of observation.

To be sure, it is always possible for an executive agency to "capture" outside groups or representatives of the media, and to make them in effect either "front organizations" or purveyors of the agency's point of view. Indeed, it is a major strategic objective of executive agencies to use outside groups in precisely this way. The leaders of interest organizations can be given quasi-official status as members of an agency's structure of advisory groups — in this way involving them to such an extent in the development of policy that they must inevitably become its defenders rather than its critics. Reporters, on the other hand, can be given preferential treatment in access to official sources, provided with advance information on pending developments, or given through "leaks" (surreptitious disclosures) inside information not available to less friendly journalists. In these and other ways some representatives of the news industry may be corrupted into a relationship of faithful adherence to official policy doctrines.

But in the end the best an executive agency can hope for is partial, not total, control of the network of outside organizations for which its activities are important. The views of interest organizations are often so various that it is not possible for an agency to develop lines of policy that will satisfy all of them simultaneously. The Department of Agriculture, for example, deals with a host of farm organizations that have competitive as well as complementary goals. Even if the leader of an interest organization can be taken into camp by an executive agency, there is no guarantee that he will be able to deliver his followers. Indeed, a trade union leader who hews too closely to the view of executive officials on wage issues may suddenly find himself a leader emeritus.

As far as reporters are concerned, they are — at least in the United States — strongly resistant to a captive role in their relations with executive agencies. For one thing, American journalists have a status of parity with government officials that reporters abroad seldom enjoy. This high standing gives them a professional pride that insures a measure of independence in their dealings with the government. Moreover, in accordance with the "muckraking" tradition of American politics, the reporter in this country ordinarily conceives of his or her appropriate role as that of exposing the misdeeds of public officials, and this role perception is itself a strong inhibition against subservience to the government.

Finally, representatives of the media as a group commonly cultivate an attitude of cynical disbelief toward statements and activities at "city hall" — a term embracing executive agencies at all levels of government. This attitude creates a built-in "credibility gap" of substantial dimensions between media personnel and government officials, and strongly reinforces the independence of reporters. True, reporters are sometimes manipulated by executive agencies into disseminating policy viewpoints that the agency wants the public to accept. They may become in effect mouthpieces for the officials or agencies they cover. At the same time, however, there is no more effective instrument than the news media for ferreting out information that agencies are trying to conceal because it contradicts the tenets of official policy.[8]

This ability to expose information that agencies would prefer to conceal makes news organizations a potential threat to the power of bureaucracy. And yet it is also true that the media can augment the power of agencies by providing them with channels through which they can reach and mobilize the support of a constituency. The reporters' hunger for news — a commodity essential to the performance of their professional task — makes them very vulnerable to being used by an agency to disseminate information that will reflect favorably upon it. The public information or public relations personnel of executive agencies have this as one of their chief functions — to feed the media stories that will enhance the public standing of their agencies. An agency may also use the media to release, or more likely, leak information damaging to another organization with which it is competing in a struggle over jurisdiction or some other bureaucratic resource.

While agencies and the media thus have a common stake in the dissemination of news, they differ radically in their perception of what should be disclosed, and this difference is at the root of much of the antagonism that crops up between the media and the bureaucracy. The news that reporters commonly seek is information that agencies are reluctant to divulge, since it contains items that cast them in an unfavorable light. What public officials would of course most prefer is for reporters to let them decide what information should be released. When, as is sometimes the case, reporters are willing to accept so passive a role for themselves, the media function not as a control over bureaucratic power, but as a major conduit through which it is exercised.

But even if this kind of capture does not take place, other factors may weaken the role of the media as a constraint upon bureaucratic power. At the national and even more at the state and local level of government, reporters often pay very little attention to the activities of executive agencies. Delmer Dunn, for example, found that reporters in Wisconsin spend most of their time covering legislators, in spite of the fact that administrative agencies are at the center of policy-making in that state as elsewhere.[9] Reporters seek out stories of general interest to a mass audience, while bureaus commonly deal with specialized subjects that reporters have neither the time nor the energy to master.

Still, Dunn also discovered that administrators much more than legislators look to the media for clues as to the character of public attitudes. Legislators tend to feel they have a direct pipeline to public opinion through elections and continuing contacts with their constituents. Executive agencies are somewhat more isolated from the public and rely on the press to a much greater extent to mirror public opinion for them — a reliance that cannot help but give the press an influence over their behavior and decisions.

Judicial Control Over Administration. The role of the judicial elite in restraining the power of bureaucrats varies from one policy sector to another. In many areas of policy, the decisions of executive agencies can be appealed to the courts. The possibility of such appeal is the greatest with respect to regulatory agencies, since their decisions may have so negative an effect upon the constitutionally protected rights of individual citizens to life, liberty, and property. An agency like the Department of State, on the other hand, may — except for passport cases — seldom have occasion to find itself in court. But the possibility of being haled before a judge and having their decisions overruled exists and represents some kind of check for all executive agencies.

Reform groups in particular have begun to use the courts as a means of controlling bureaucratic decisions and behavior. In the early part of this century, the courts were looked upon by reformers as hidebound institutions that blocked social and economic change by insisting upon due process of law and being excessively preoccupied with the protection of property rights. In modern times, however, the reform perspective has shifted. Reformers today routinely go to court to challenge decisions by executive agencies that they regard as damaging to the public interest, or to force agencies to use powers to protect the public that are lying dormant in their hands. Where once they were seen as obstacles to change, the courts have now become major channels through which reform groups can pursue their goals in areas like environmental and consumer protection.

To be sure, there is a vast area of administrative action that is, in legal parlance, nonreviewable. Partly this is attributable to legal considerations, such as the fact that much of administrative policymaking does not generate cases or controversies that can be taken to court. Partly, however, it rests upon considerations of prudence. When an agency has a continuing relationship of supervision with respect to a private organization or individual, this relationship often breeds acquiescence even to agency actions that are regarded as challengeable in court, since the agency's capacity for reprisal deters assaults upon its authority.[10]

Moreover, the outlook is not always promising for individuals who choose to contest agency actions in court. On balance, it is more favorable in state and local than it is in national administration, since judges at these lower echelons have tended to construe the powers of government more narrowly than jurists in the federal court system. From a study of the U.S. Supreme Court decisions with respect to ten executive agencies over the decade 1947–56, Joseph Tanenhaus concluded that "the Court and its individual members favor federal agencies more frequently than they oppose them to a statistically significant degree." [11]

At all levels of government, one of the most important effects of judicial review of administrative decisions is to enlarge the role and influence of lawyers in the policy-making process within bureaucracy. Since advice on the legality of proposed courses of action is their specialty, lawyers are in a position to discourage certain policy measures they consider undesirable by declaring that these policies are certain to invoke judicial veto.[12]

The structure of influence over decision-making within executive agencies is thus affected by the fact that bureaucrats share power in the policy process with outside elites. Moreover, lawyers are not the only group inside bureaucracy who benefit from the necessity of negotiating with external forces. The role of budget officers in policy decisions is buttressed by the fact that they play a primary role in the bargaining with political elites that is necessary to obtain fiscal resources. The influence of legislative liaison officials in an executive agency is derived in no small measure from their close association with the legislators whose good-will is vital to the agency's development and even survival. And public information officers can use their intimate contacts with outside groups and the news media to expand their own influence in policy deliberations within bureaucracy. The participation of outside elites in the policy process thus has a major effect not only upon the nature of the decisions made within executive organizations, but also upon the identity of those who make these decisions.

The Inner Check

Limitations upon the power of bureaucracy stem not only from the competitive pressures of nonbureaucratic elites but also from factors related to the way in which organizations operate and bureaucrats behave within their own habitat. Even if there were no forces in the external environment to restrict their power, executive agencies would still find themselves limited in the scope of their discretion and the extent of their influence by restraints originating in the internal life of bureaucracy itself.

Competition Among Bureaucracies. Not least important in this respect is the struggle for primacy that is so constant a characteristic of the relations among executive agencies. While the overt objective of this struggle is to strengthen the agencies that participate in it, an unanticipated consequence of such interbureaucratic combat is that the agencies involved become much more susceptible to outside control.

In the United States, for example, the various branches of the armed forces have long engaged in vigorous competition for financial support as well as jurisdiction over various weapons systems and combat missions. While this interservice rivalry was weakened by the amalgamation of the separate services into a single military establishment in the Department of Defense, it was not ended. This competition has played an important role in facilitating civilian control over the military primarily because it has forced each branch of the service into searching criticism of the defense policies advocated by the others, thus preventing the emergence of a monolithic military point of view on national security matters and enabling outside groups to make their own influence felt by siding with one military organization or another.

American presidents, for example, have never had much difficulty in finding support among military organizations for whatever defense policies the chief executives wished to adopt.[13] On one occasion, a president was even able to use the views of a foreign bureaucracy as a counter-weight to the recommendations of his own military establishment. Early in World War II, President Franklin D. Roosevelt came under strong pressure from the American armed forces to authorize the establishment of a second front in Europe. He was aided substantially in his resistance to this pressure by simultaneous opposition to such a venture from the British military organizations with which the American high command was then in close consultation.[14]

Competition as a restraint upon bureaucratic power functions within executive agencies as well as between them, in the form of a struggle for power among the various professional groups that play a role in the operation of a single agency. As earlier discussion has shown, there are multiple forms of expertise in bureaucratic organizations in advanced industrial societies, and there are many areas of policy deliberation within these organizations where decisions are shaped by competitive pressures from different clusters of professionals.

In modern American bureaucracy the role of such natural rivalries in controlling bureaucratic behavior has been supplemented by the deliberate creation of executive organizations whose major function is that of monitoring the decisions of other agencies to see that they conform to certain specified policy goals. The Commission on Civil Rights, for example, has the task of seeing to it that national agencies do not discriminate against women, blacks, and other disadvantaged groups in their personnel policies, and the reports of the commission have often been severely critical of the practices of various agencies in this regard. In a similar way the Environmental Protection Agency (EPA) seeks to have all executive agencies abide by standards designed to protect the natural environment from deterioration resulting from, among other things, air or water pollution. Both the Commission on Civil Rights and EPA thus function as what might be called adversary bureaucracies — set up to bring the decisions and actions of other agencies under greater security and to deter them from malpractices.[15]

One form of adversary organization that has been much used in European societies to control bureaucracy is the office of the *ombudsman* — an administrative agency charged to help citizens obtain remedies for decisions by executive officials that inflict unjustified injury upon them. This institution, developed initially in Sweden, has spread to many other countries as well, and it is being increasingly urged as the solution to the problem of controlling the unwarranted exercise of bureaucratic power in all societies. One of the major factors leading to the creation of the ombudsman office is the expectation that it will make agency decisions more sensitive to the needs and interests of individuals whose circumstances may not always fit neatly into the classes or groups into which bureaucrats tend to categorize the population.[16]

Internalized Restraints. Perhaps the truest kind of "inner check" upon bureaucratic power is not interagency rivalry, which requires, after all, a vigorously competitive relationship between two or more executive organizations, but restraints that operate within the personalities of bureaucrats themselves — preventing them from unlawful or excessive use of the power placed in their keeping. Such internalized restraints have as their great advantage the fact that, when they are effective, they operate as a constant presence — exercising a restraining influence in areas of decision known perhaps only to the bureaucrat himself.

Ideally, the bureaucrat's conception of his own role in the governing process can be structured to constitute by itself a substantial check upon the extravagant use of his power.[17] If bureaucrats themselves feel it is necessary to defer to the preferences of citizens in framing public policy, or regard it as reprehensible to use power in ways that infringe upon the liberties of individuals subject to their jurisdiction, then the problem of controlling bureaucratic power is very largely solved at the source. Inhibitions on the part of the bureaucrat may in this case serve as an effective substitute for external controls.

Significant in this respect is the fact that codes of ethics adopted by administrative groups such as city managers characteristically accept a subordinate role for bureaucrats in the governmental process. To be sure this acceptance may be mere lip service, designed to disguise the extent to which city managers as well as other bureaucrats actually control policy decisions. At the same time, however, it seems fair to assume that there will always be some strain toward consistency on the part of administrative officials, and that a bureaucrat's conception of his role as a limited one will have a restraining effect upon his behavior in office.

Certainly it is true that in a country like the United States, bureaucrats are, like all other citizens, subject to processes of education as children, and of continuing indoctrination as adults, that stress the importance of adherence to fair play in the relations between government and the citizen, as well as the obligation of public officials to defer to the will of the people.[18] And if bureaucrats were to forget the fact that their proper role is that of the public's servant and not its master, a variety of institutions —including legislative bodies, the courts, and the press — would be quick to remind them of the subordinate nature of their role.

Moreover, many executive agencies have developed their own ways of keeping themselves in touch with public opinion. They follow the results of public opinion surveys taken by polling organizations or may even conduct their own polls. Agencies may also monitor editorials in newspapers on the policy issues with which they are concerned, as well as letters to the editor. They can also respond to complaints filed with the special service some segments of the media now provide where citizens may send in complaints about a grievance they have for which an administrative agency may be responsible, or be able to provide a remedy. Through these and other techniques, agencies may establish direct links with public opinion, and thus acquire a capacity to "anticipate the reactions" of the public in designing official policy.[19]

Of course, a system under which executive officials themselves take public opinion into account in their policy decisions differs from a genuine system of representation or citizen participation where the public has an opportunity to speak for itself either directly, or through officials it elects. When public opinion only filters into executive agencies through the lens of bureaucratic perceptions, the image that emerges may be grossly distorted — reflecting not the actual contours of opinion but the image that it is convenient for the bureaucrat to see.[20]

There has been a long-standing dispute in the literature of public administration as to whether the more effective way of containing the expansion of bureaucratic power is through the various internal restraints just discussed or through the competition among elites outlined in the earlier sections of this chapter. The argument for the primacy of the inner checks rests essentially on the grounds that these controls operate more pervasively and effectively than the efforts at surveillance of bureaucratic behavior by external elites. Given the complexity of modern government, it is impossible to avoid leaving large amounts of power in the hands of bureaucrats to be used at their discretion.

However, the chief disadvantage of these purely psychological inner checks is that they rely essentially upon the inculcation of virtue, operating through either conscientious scruples on the part of the individual official, or a code of honor or ethics prevailing among an administrative group to which a bureaucrat feels he must conform. But as Herman Finer has pointed out, "reliance on an official's conscience may be reliance on an official's accomplice," since "the political and administrative history of all ages . . . has demonstrated without the shadow of a doubt that sooner or later there is an abuse of power when external punitive controls are lacking."[21]

The competition among elites, on the other hand, rests upon the solid bedrock of human selfishness — the ambition of political and

bureaucratic elites alike to pursue and protect their own power interests. It was just such motives as these that the authors of *The
Federalist Papers* saw as the most dependable base on which restraints on power could be built realistically into the American
constitutional system: "Ambition must be made to counteract ambition. The interest of the man must be connected with the constitutional rights of the place . . . the constant aim is to divide and
arrange the several offices in such a manner as that each may be a
check on the other — that the private interest of every individual
may be a sentinel over the public rights." [22]

A Representative Bureaucracy. It has long been felt, not only in
the United States but in other countries as well, that the surest way
of insuring that a bureaucracy will be responsive in its inner heart
to a community is to require it to recruit personnel so that it is
representative of that community in the composition of its membership. Thus, throughout American history there has been a continuing effort to open up employment opportunities in bureaucracy
to all segments of the country. In part this effort has been motivated
by a commitment to equality of economic opportunity. In the
United States as elsewhere, public bureaucracy has become an increasingly significant source of jobs. Indeed in underdeveloped
countries, bureaucracy is often the only major employer in the
society.

But beyond this commitment to equal economic opportunity,
there is the belief that a bureaucracy which mirrors a society in its
social, economic, and cultural composition will be much more
sensitive to the needs of citizens of that society, and much less
likely to be arbitrary or abusive when it is exercising power over
"its own kind" of people. It is this sort of premise that lies behind
the recruitment of blacks to urban police departments in the
United States today, for example, but since at least the days of
President Andrew Jackson the idea of a representative bureaucracy
has had great appeal in the United States as a logical implication of
the American commitment to democracy itself.

This representative bureaucracy concept has been strongly criticized when it has appeared to conflict with the modern attachment
to the standard of merit in recruiting public servants — the belief
that preferment should be given in all decisions regarding public
employment to the most able and qualified applicants in society. In

this connection, as in other ways noted earlier, steps taken to insure a more responsive bureaucracy often come into apparent conflict with the need to maintain the effectiveness of public agencies. A compromise sometimes reached in a number of countries — including the United States and Israel — is to adhere to the standard of merit in filling certain positions where skill is an indispensable requirement in public bureaucracy, but to attempt to satisfy the need for representation of all segments of society in recruiting for other positions requiring somewhat less technical skill.[23]

The quest for a representative bureaucracy can help to achieve other goals besides economic and political equality. One very important role it can play is that of helping to overcome divisions and alienation within a society—especially one as fragmented as the United States. In the days of Jackson prior to the Civil War, access to public employment helped to overcome friction between inhabitants of the newly settled regions in the West and the more established Eastern Seaboard area. After the Civil War, the assimilation of newly arrived immigrant groups — as, for example, the Irish — was greatly facilitated by the availability of jobs in the public sector, especially in the large cities where immigrants tended to cluster. In contemporary American culture, public employment has come to play an increasingly important role in satisfying the aspirations of various disadvantaged groups, especially blacks. In appraising the value of representation as a goal in recruiting public servants, it is important to remember that it can serve latent functions like political integration as well as more manifest egalitarian objectives.

THE ENDURING PROBLEM OF BUREAUCRACY

Extensive as the controls over bureaucracy may seem to be, both from external and internal sources, the power of executive officials yet remains an object of intense concern in modern politics. To some extent this anxiety reflects the persistent strength of a political mythology in many countries that credits bureaucracy with a good deal more power than it actually has. It needs also to be remembered that while the power of bureaucracy is so often seen as a threat to the traditional freedoms of a democratic society, this power can also be used to protect and extend those freedoms.

As one notable case in point, the U.S. Commission on Civil

Rights is a bureaucracy that has as its chief purpose the task of seeing to it that minority citizens are not denied the rights guaranteed them by the constitution, and it is not the only executive agency that plays such a role. Moreover, as previously noted, when the Nixon administration began carrying on the illegal and covert activities that were eventually to lead to its removal from office, it became clear that bureaucratic organizations could sometimes help to strengthen rather than weaken democracy by exposing if not actually opposing the plans of their political superiors.

At the same time neither the Watergate episode nor any other recent development can erase the fact that a decisive power of initiative now lies in the hands of career bureaucrats. Apprehensions over the power of executive agencies are well-grounded in the realities of modern politics. There is, for example, always the nightmarish possibility that military organizations may use their power over the disposition and use of weapons to precipitate a thermonuclear war that would destroy modern civilization. Against such a holocaust, the controls already discussed in this chapter may seem pitifully inadequate, even though the outbreak of war today is as likely to stem from the miscalculations of politicians, or the passions of the public, as it is from precipitous actions on the part of bureaucrats.

Fear of bureaucracy is not altogether relieved by the fact that public agencies do not wield monopoly power, but are linked instead in a policy system with other bureaucratic or nonbureaucratic elites. The fact of the matter is that relations among these groups can more closely resemble oligopoly than they do competition. This is to say that these separate elites may be able to find common interests in the development of policies that will satisfy all their distinct interests simultaneously. The military-industrial complex in the United States, for example, is often identified as just such an arrangement under which military bureaucracies, defense contractors in private industry, and political elites, such as congressmen concerned with military affairs, are linked together in the support of a high level of defense spending from which each group derives substantial benefits. In a situation of this sort, the belief that outside elites will serve as effective instruments of restraint upon a government agency may be an illusory expectation.

If there is one factor that contributes more than any other to bureaucratic dominance in the political system, it is inattention on the part of the other actors or participants in policy-making, who have at least the potential capacity to limit the influence bureaucrats can exert over government actions or decisions.

This inattention may result from the practices of secrecy that executive agencies so often follow with respect to policy decisions or deliberations — especially in the area of national security affairs. People can hardly be attentive to matters about which they are allowed to know nothing. Secrecy may thus serve bureaucratic power by enforcing inattention to important policy issues on the part of other participants in political life.

The complexity of many of the issues with which bureaucracies deal may also reduce if not foreclose attention by other political actors. It is difficult for many of these actors to invest the time necessary to understand the issues that executive agencies commonly confront, and complexity is increasingly a characteristic of the policy issues that arise on the agenda of contemporary politics. Both secrecy and complexity thus work in much the same way to prevent other participants in the policy process from giving attention to decisions that bureaucratic organizations may be making.

A crisis in policy makes dramatically clear the degree to which bureaucratic power thrives on the inattention of other participants in the policy process. In a crisis, for example, the president gives close and continuous attention to an area of policy that he would ordinarily leave to the discretion of his subordinates. The public may be momentarily aroused and pay what is for it unusual attention to a policy issue. Eventually, however, the crisis atmosphere recedes, and as policy-making falls back into obscurity, it once again tends to be dominated by the routines of bureaucracy.

The future will thus present a continuing challenge to find techniques for maintaining effective oversight over the exercise of bureaucratic power. In the past, democratic societies have exhibited impressive powers of invention in this regard. The development of public interest organizations in contemporary American politics suggests that this inventive capacity is still very strong. However, a variety of circumstances in modern life, as, for example, the growing weight of expert knowledge in policy formation, continue to push bureaucracy toward a position of preeminence in the governing process. As we have seen, this bureaucratic power rests partly on the extraordinary capacities of public agencies as sources of expertise, but partly also on the fact that administrative agencies have become major centers for the mobilization of political energy and support. As a result, bureaucratic politics rather than party politics has become the dominant theater of decision in the modern state. The adjustment of democratic society to this fact continues to demand all the resourceful ingenuity of which it is capable.

Notes

1. For an analysis of some of the early literature bearing on this problem, see Dwight Waldo, *The Administrative State* (New York: The Ronald Press, 1948), pp. 89–103.
2. See pp. 83–84, 90.
3. David Riesman, *The Lonely Crowd* (New Haven: Yale University Press, 1950), p. 252.
4. See J. Leiper Freeman, *The Political Process: Executive Bureau — Legislative Committee Relations* (New York: Random House, rev. ed., 1965), pp. 80–81.
5. In this connection, see the account of the career of Representative Carl Vinson of Georgia in David B. Truman, *The Governmental Process* (New York: Alfred A. Knopf, 1951), p. 424.
6. For an analysis of the role of private business organizations in framing public policy in the United States, see Mark V. Nadel, "The Hidden Dimension of Public Policy: Private Governments and the Policy Making Process," *Journal of Politics* 37 (February 1975): 2–34.
7. See, in this connection, Douglass Cater, *The Fourth Branch of Government* (Boston: Houghton Mifflin Co., 1959).
8. Analyses of the many-sided relationship between executive agencies and the press may be found in Cater, *The Fourth Branch,* Bernard Cohen, *The Press and Foreign Policy* (Princeton, N.J.: Princeton University Press, 1963), Dan Nimmo, *Newsgathering in Washington* (New York: Atherton Press, 1964), William L. Rivers, *The Opinionmakers* (Boston: Beacon Press, 1965), and Leon V. Sigal, *Reporters and Officials* (Lexington, Mass.: Lexington Books, D. C. Heath and Co., 1973).
9. Delmer D. Dunn, *Public Officials and the Press* (Reading, Mass.: Addison-Wesley, 1969).
10. See also the discussion on this point on p. 36.
11. See Joseph Tanenhaus, "Supreme Court Attitudes Toward Federal Administrative Agencies," *The Journal of Politics* 22 (August 1960): 513. Out of 243 decisions involving federal agencies, 168 were favorable to them.
12. For an informative account of the role of lawyers in bureaucratic policymaking, see Victor A. Thompson, *The Regulatory Process in OPA Rationing* (New York: Columbia University Press, 1950), esp. pp. 207–22.
13. See Samuel P. Huntington, *The Common Defense* (New York: Columbia University Press, 1961), pp. 371–72, 113–15.

14. See, in this regard, William R. Emerson, "F.D.R.," in Ernest R. May, ed., *The Ultimate Decision: The President as Commander in Chief* (New York: George Braziller, 1960), pp. 135–77.

15. An organization that has long functioned in much the same way to monitor the fiscal policies and practices of other executive agencies in the United States is the General Accounting Office. Another agency presently being proposed, the Consumer Protection Agency, would have the role of speaking for consumer interests in proceedings before other regulatory bodies in the executive branch when they make decisions affecting the consuming public.

16. The role of the ombudsman has attracted growing attention in the literature of comparative administration. See especially Walter Gellhorn, *Ombudsman and Others: Citizens' Protectors in Nine Countries* (Cambridge: Harvard University Press, 1967), and Donald C. Rowat, *The Ombudsman Plan: Essays on the Worldwide Spread of an Idea.* (Toronto: McClelland and Stewart, 1973).

17. The term role is here used in the sense of forms of behaviors expected of, or considered suitable for, individuals occupying a certain position or performing a particular function in an organization. See Abraham Zaleznik, "Interpersonal Relations in Organizations," in James March, ed., *Handbook of Organizations* (Chicago: Rand McNally and Co., 1965), pp. 589–90.

18. However, a survey of bureaucrats found that about one-third of them agreed with a variety of antidemocratic statements on, for example, freedom of speech. See Bob L. Wynia, "Federal Bureaucrats' Attitudes Toward a Democratic Ideology," *Public Administration Review* 34 (March/April 1974): 156–62.

19. The concept of "anticipated reactions" to describe the way in which public opinion is built into the original design of policy comes from Carl Friedrich, "Public Policy and the Nature of Administrative Responsibility," in Carl J. Friedrich and Edward S. Mason, eds., *Public Policy* (Cambridge: Harvard University Press, 1940), pp. 15–16.

20. See, for example, the description of the "trustee" relationship between administrative officials and their public in Robert S. Friedman, Bernard W. Klein, and John H. Romani, "Administrative Agencies and the Publics They Serve," *Public Administration Review* XXVI (September 1966): 195: "a trustee . . . is satisfied with the knowledge that his constituents are supportive of his decisions and is likely to read the absence of complaints by constituents as support or acceptance."

21. Herman Finer, "Administrative Responsibility in Democratic Government," *Public Administration Review* I (Summer 1941): 336–37.

22. See Roy P. Fairfield, ed., *The Federalist Papers* (Garden City, N.Y.: Doubleday Anchor edition, 1961), p. 160.

23. For a discussion of these trade-offs as they have occurred in a number of societies, see Samuel Krislov, *Representative Bureaucracy* (Englewood Cliffs, N.J.: Prentice-Hall, 1974), esp. pp. 82–103. Cf. also V. Subramanian, "Representative Bureaucracy: A Reassessment," *American Political Science Review* LXI (December 1967): 1010–19.

Selected Bibliography

Albrow, Martin. *Bureaucracy.* New York: Praeger, 1970.

Allison, Graham T. *Essence of Decision: Explaining the Cuban Missile Crisis.* Boston: Little, Brown and Co., 1971.

Altshuler, Alan A. *Community Control.* New York: Pegasus, 1970.

Anderson, Patrick. *The Presidents' Men.* New York: Doubleday & Co., 1969.

Bachrach, Peter, and Morton S. Baratz. *Power and Poverty.* New York: Oxford University Press, 1970.

Banfield, Edward C. *Political Influence.* New York: Free Press of Glencoe, 1961.

Bell, Daniel. *The Coming of Post-Industrial Society.* New York: Basic Books, 1973.

Benjamin, Gerald. *Race Relations and the New York City Commission on Human Rights.* Ithaca, N.Y.: Cornell University Press, 1974.

Bennis, Warren G. *Changing Organizations.* New York: McGraw Hill, 1966.

Benveniste, Guy. *The Politics of Expertise.* Berkeley: The Glendessary Press, 1972.

Bernstein, Marver H. *Regulating Business by Independent Commission.* Princeton, N.J.: Princeton University Press, 1955.

————. *The Job of the Federal Executive.* Washington: The Brookings Institution, 1958.

Braybrooke, David, and Charles E. Lindblom. *A Strategy of Decision.* New York: Free Press of Glencoe, 1963.

Brown, MacAlister. "The Demise of State Department Public Opinion Polls: A Study in Legislative Oversight," *Midwest Journal of Political Science* V (February 1961): 1–17.

Caiden, Gerald E. *Administrative Reform.* Chicago: Aldine, 1969.

Cater, Douglass. *The Fourth Branch of Government.* Boston: Houghton Mifflin Co., 1959.

Clark, Burton R. "Organizational Adaptation and Precarious Values: A Case Study," *American Sociological Review* 21 (June 1956): 327–36.

Cohen, Bernard. *The Press and Foreign Policy.* Princeton, N.J.: Princeton University Press, 1963.

Corson, John J., and R. Shale Paul. *Men Near the Top.* Baltimore: The Johns Hopkins Press, 1966.

Crenson, Matthew A. *The Unpolitics of Air Pollution.* Baltimore: The Johns Hopkins Press, 1971.

————. *The Federal Machine: Beginnings of Bureaucracy in Jacksonian America.* Baltimore: The Johns Hopkins Press, 1975.

Cronin, Thomas E., and Sanford D. Greenberg. *The Presidential Advisory System.* New York: Harper and Row, 1969.

Crozier, Michel. *The Bureaucratic Phenomenon.* Chicago: University of Chicago Press, 1964.

Dahl, Robert A. *Who Governs?* New Haven: Yale University Press, 1961.

————, and Charles E. Lindblom. *Politics, Economics, and Welfare.* New York: Harper & Bros., 1953.

Davidson, Roger H. "Congress and the Executive: The Race for Representation." In Alfred DeGrazia, coord., *Twelve Studies of the Organization of Congress.* Washington, D.C.: The American Enterprise Institute for Public Policy Research, 1966.

Davis, David. *How the Bureaucracy Makes Foreign Policy: An Exchange Analysis.* Lexington, Mass.: Lexington Books, D. C. Heath and Co., 1972.

Davis, James W., Jr., and Kenneth Dolbeare. *Little Groups of Neighbors: The Selective Service System.* Chicago: Markham Publishing Co., 1968.

Davis, Kenneth C. *Discretionary Justice.* Baton Rouge: Louisiana State University Press, 1969.

Destler, I. M. *Presidents, Bureaucrats, and Foreign Policy.* Princeton: Princeton University Press, 1972.

Downs, Anthony. *Inside Bureaucracy.* Boston: Little, Brown and Co., 1967.

————. "Up and Down with Ecology — the Issue Attention Cycle," *The Public Interest* 28 (Summer 1972): 38–50.

Dror, Yehezkel. "Muddling Through — 'Science' or Inertia?," *Public Administration Review* XXIV (September 1964): 153–57.

————. "Policy Analysts: A New Professional Role in Government Service," *Public Administration Review* XXVII (September 1967):197–203.

Dunn, Delmer D. *Public Officials and the Press.* Reading, Mass.: Addison-Wesley, 1969.

Dvorin, Eugene P., and Robert H. Simmons. *From Amoral to Humane Bureaucracy.* San Francisco: The Canfield Press, 1972.

Edelman, Murray. *The Symbolic Uses of Politics.* Urbana, Ill.: The University of Illinois Press, 1964.

Eisenstadt, Samuel N. "Bureaucracy and Bureaucratization." In *Essays on Comparative Institutions.* New York: John Wiley & Sons, 1965, pp. 175–271.

Etzioni, Amitai. *A Comparative Analysis of Complex Organizations.* New York: Free Press of Glencoe, 1961.

————. *Modern Organizations.* Englewood Cliffs, N.J.: Prentice-Hall, 1964.

————. "Mixed-Scanning: A 'Third' Approach to Decision-Making," *Public Administration Review* XXVII (December 1967): 385–92.

Fainsod, Merle. "Some Reflections on the Nature of the Regulatory Process." In Carl J. Friedrich and Edward S. Mason, eds., *Public Policy.* Vol. I. Cambridge: Harvard University Press, 1940.

Falk, Stanley L. "The National Security Council Under Truman, Eisenhower, and Kennedy," *Political Science Quarterly* LXXIX (September 1964): 403–34.

Feit, Edward. *The Armed Bureaucrats.* Boston: Houghton Mifflin Co., 1973.

Fenno, Richard F. *The Power of the Purse.* Boston: Little, Brown and Co., 1966.

————. *The President's Cabinet.* Cambridge: Harvard University Press, 1959.

Ferkiss, Victor C. *Technological Man.* New York: George Brazeller, Inc., 1969.

Finer, Herman. "Administrative Responsibility in Democratic Government," *Public Administration Review* I (Summer 1941): 335–50.

Fisher, Louis. *President and Congress.* New York: The Free Press, 1972.

Flash, Edward S., Jr. *Economic Advice and Presidential Leadership.* New York: Columbia University Press, 1965.

Foss, Phillip O. *Politics and Grass.* Seattle: University of Washington Press, 1960.

Fox, Douglas M. *The Politics of City and State Bureaucracy.* Pacific Palisades, Calif.: Goodyear Publishing Co., 1974.

Franck, Thomas M., and Edward Weisband, eds. *Secrecy and Foreign Policy.* New York: Oxford University Press, 1974.

Freeman, J. Leiper. *The Political Process: Executive Bureau-Legislative Committee Relations.* New York: Random House, rev. ed., 1965.

————. "The Bureaucracy in Pressure Politics," *Annals* of the American Academy of Political and Social Science 319 (September 1958): 10–19.

Friedman, Robert S. *Professionalism: Expertise and Policy Making.* New York: The General Learning Press, 1971.

————, Bernard W. Klein, and John H. Romani. "Administrative Agencies and the Publics They Serve," *Public Administration Review* XXVI (September 1966): 192–204.

Friedrich, Carl J. "Public Policy and the Nature of Administrative Responsibility." In Carl J. Friedrich and Edward S. Mason, eds., *Public Policy* I. Cambridge: Harvard University Press, 1940.

Gawthrop, Louis C. *Administrative Politics and Social Change*. New York: St. Martin's Press, 1971.

Gellhorn, Ernest. "Adverse Publicity by Administrative Agencies," *Harvard Law Review* 86 (June 1973): 1380–1441.

George, Alexander M. "The Case for Multiple Advocacy in Making Foreign Policy," *American Political Science Review* LXVI (September 1972): 751–85.

Gerth, H. H., and C. Wright Mills. *From Max Weber: Essays in Sociology*. New York: Oxford University Press, 1946, pp. 196–244.

Gilb, Corinne L. *Hidden Hierarchies*. New York: Harper and Row, 1966.

Gilbert, Charles E. "The Framework of Administrative Responsibility," *Journal of Politics* 21 (August 1959): 373–407.

Gilmour, Robert S. "Central Legislative Clearance: A Revised Perspective," *Public Administration Review* XXXI (March/April 1971): 150–58.

Gilpin, Robert, and Christopher Wright, eds. *Scientists and National Policy-Making*. New York: Columbia University Press, 1964.

Green, Philip. "Science, Government and the Case of RAND: A Singular Pluralism," *World Politics* XX (January 1968): 301–26.

Greenberg, Daniel S. *The Politics of Pure Science*. New York: New American Library, 1968.

Haar, John E. *The Professional Diplomat*. Princeton, N.J.: Princeton University Press, 1969.

Halberstam, David. *The Best and the Brightest*. New York: Random House, 1972.

Halperin, Morton H. "The Gaither Committee and the Policy Process," *World Politics* XIII (April 1961): 360–84.

————. *Bureaucratic Politics and Foreign Policy*. Washington, D.C.: The Brookings Institution, 1974.

Hammond, Paul Y. "The National Security Council as a Device for Interdepartmental Coordination," *American Political Science Review* LIV (December 1960): 899–910.

————. "Foreign Policy-Making and Administrative Politics," *World Politics* XVII (July 1965): 656–71.

Hardin, Charles M. *The Politics of Agriculture*. Glencoe, Ill.: The Free Press, 1952.

Hargrove, Erwin C. *The Missing Link: The Study of the Implementation of Social Policy.* Washington, D.C.: The Urban Institute, 1975.

Harris, Joseph P. *Congressional Control of Administration.* New York: Doubleday Anchor edition, 1965.

Hershey, Gary. *Protest in the Public Service.* Lexington, Mass.: Lexington Books, D. C. Heath and Co., 1973.

Heyman, Victor K. "Government by Contract: Boon or Boner?," *Public Administration Review* XXI (Spring 1961): 59–64.

Hilsman, Roger. "Congressional-Executive Relations and the Foreign Policy Consensus," *American Political Science Review* LII (September 1958): 725–44.

Hirschman, Albert O. *Exit, Voice, and Loyalty.* Cambridge: Harvard University Press, 1970.

Hitch, Charles J. *Decision-Making for Defense.* Berkeley and Los Angeles: University of California Press, 1965.

Holden, Matthew, Jr. " 'Imperialism' in Bureaucracy," *American Political Science Review* LX (December 1966): 943–51.

Huntington, Samuel P. "The Marasmus of the I.C.C.: The Commission, the Railroads, and the Public Interest," *Yale Law Journal* 61 (April 1952): 467–509.

————. *The Soldier and the State.* Cambridge: Harvard University Press, 1957.

————. *The Common Defense: Strategic Programs in National Politics.* New York: Columbia University Press, 1961.

Jacob, Charles E. *Policy and Bureaucracy.* New York: D. Van Nostrand, 1966.

Jacob, Herbert, and Kenneth N. Vines, eds. *Politics in the American States.* Boston: Little, Brown and Co., 1971.

Janis, Irving L. *Victims of Groupthink.* Boston: Houghton Mifflin Co., 1972.

Janowitz, Morris. *The Professional Soldier.* New York: Free Press of Glencoe, 1960.

Jennings, M. Kent. *Community Influentials.* New York: Free Press of Glencoe, 1964.

————, Milton C. Cummings, Jr., and Franklin P. Kilpatrick. "Trusted Leaders: Perceptions of Appointed Federal Officials," *Public Opinion Quarterly* 30 (Fall 1966): 368–84.

Jones, Charles O. *An Introduction to the Study of Public Policy.* Belmont, Calif.: Wadsworth Publishing Co., 1970.

————. "The Limits of Public Support: Air Pollution Agency Development," *Public Administration Review* XXXII (September/October 1972): 502–8.

Kaufman, Herbert. "Emerging Conflicts in the Doctrines of Public Administration," *American Political Science Review* L (December 1956): 1057–73.

———. *The Forest Ranger.* Baltimore: The Johns Hopkins Press, 1960.

———. *Administrative Feedback: Monitoring Subordinates' Behavior.* Washington, D.C.: The Brookings Institution, 1973.

Keiser, Norman F. "Public Responsibility and Federal Advisory Groups: A Case Study," *Western Political Quarterly* XI (June 1958): 251–64.

Kerr, James R. "Congress and Space: Overview or Oversight?," *Public Administration Review* XXV (September 1965): 185–92.

Knorr, Klaus. "Failures in National Intelligence Estimates: The Case of the Cuban Missiles," *World Politics* XVI (April 1964): 455–67.

Kohlmeier, Louis M. *The Regulators.* New York: Harper and Row, 1969.

Krislov, Samuel. *Representative Bureaucracy.* Englewood Cliffs, N.J.: Prentice-Hall, 1974.

Kroll, Morton. "Hypotheses and Designs for the Study of Public Policies in the United States," *Midwest Journal of Political Science* VI (November 1962): 363–83.

Landau, Martin. "Redundancy, Rationality, and the Problem of Duplication and Overlap," *Public Administration Review* 29 (July/August 1969): 346–58.

La Palombara, Joseph, ed. *Bureaucracy and Political Development.* Princeton: Princeton University Press, 1963.

Leiserson, Avery. "Political Limitations on Executive Reorganization," *American Political Science Review* XLI (February 1947): 68–84.

———. "Scientists and the Policy Process," *American Political Science Review* LIX (June 1965): 408–16.

Levine, Sol, and Paul E. White. "Exchange as a Conceptual Framework for the Study of Interorganizational Relationships," *Administrative Science Quarterly* 5 (March 1961): 583–601.

Lindblom, Charles E. "Policy Analysis," *American Economic Review* 48 (June 1958): 298–312.

———. *The Intelligence of Democracy.* New York: Free Press of Glencoe, 1965.

Long, Norton. *The Polity.* Chicago: Rand McNally & Co., 1962.

Lowi, Theodore J. "American Business, Public Policy, Case Studies, and Political Theory," *World Politics* XVI (July 1964): 677–715.

———. *The End of Liberalism.* New York: W. W. Norton and Co., 1969.

Maass, Arthur. *Muddy Waters.* Cambridge: Harvard University Press, 1951.

———. "Benefit-Cost Analysis: Its Relevance to Public Investment Decisions," *Quarterly Journal of Economics* LXXX (May 1966): 208–26.

McConnell, Grant. *Private Power and American Democracy.* New York: Alfred Knopf, 1966.

Macmahon, Arthur W. "Congressional Oversight of Administration: The Power of the Purse," *Political Science Quarterly* LVIII (June 1943): 161–90; (September 1943): 380–414.

Mann, Dean E. "The Selection of Federal Political Executives," *American Political Science Review* LVIII (March 1964): 81–99.

Mann, Seymour Z. "Policy Formulation in the Executive Branch: The Taft-Hartley Experience," *Western Political Quarterly* XIII (September 1960): 597–608.

March, James G., and Herbert A. Simon. *Organizations*. New York: John Wiley & Sons, 1958.

Marini, Frank, ed. *Toward the New Public Administration: The Minnowbrook Perspective*. Scranton, Pa.: The Chandler Publishing Co., 1971.

Martin, Laurence W. "The Market for Strategic Ideas in Britain: The 'Sandys Era,'" *American Political Science Review* LVI (March 1962): 23–41.

Morgan, Robert J. "Pressure Politics and Resources Administration," *Journal of Politics* 18 (February 1956): 39–60.

Mosher, Frederick C. *Democracy and the Public Service*. New York: Oxford University Press, 1968.

Nadel, Mark V. *The Politics of Consumer Protection*. Indianapolis, Ind.: The Bobbs-Merrill Co., 1971.

———. "The Hidden Dimension of Public Policy: Private Governments and the Policy Making Process," *Journal of Politics* 37 (February 1975): 2–34.

———, and Francis E. Rourke. "Bureaucracies." In Fred I. Greenstein and Nelson W. Polsby, eds., *Handbook of Political Science*. Vol. 5:373–440. Reading, Mass.: Addison-Wesley, 1975.

Neustadt, Richard E. *Presidential Power*. New York: John Wiley & Sons, 1960.

———. "Approaches to Staffing the Presidency: Notes on FDR and JFK," *American Political Science Review* LVII (December 1963): 855–64.

———. "White House and Whitehall," *The Public Interest*, no. 2 (Winter 1966): 55–69.

Nieburg, H. L. "The Eisenhower AEC and Congress: A Study in Executive-Legislative Relations," *Midwest Journal of Political Science* VI (May 1962): 115–48.

Niskanen, William A. *Bureaucracy and Representative Government*. Chicago: Aldine Atherton, 1971.

Ostrom, Vincent. *The Intellectual Crisis in American Public Administration*. University, Ala.: University of Alabama Press, 1971.

Peabody, Robert L., and Francis E. Rourke. "Public Bureaucracies." In James G. March, ed., *Handbook of Organizations*. Chicago: Rand McNally & Co., 1965.

Penniman, Clara. "Reorganization and the Internal Revenue Service," *Public Administration Review* 21 (Summer 1961): 121–30.

Pipe, G. Russell. "Congressional Liaison: The Executive Branch Consolidates Its Relations with Congress," *Public Administration Review* XXVI (March 1966): 14–24.

Polsby, Nelson W. *Congress and the Presidency*. Englewood Cliffs, N.J.: Prentice-Hall, 1971.

Posvar, Wesley W. "The Impact of Strategy Expertise on the National Security Policy of the U.S." In John D. Montgomery and Arthur Smithies, eds., *Public Policy* XIII. Cambridge: Harvard University Press, 1964.

Pressman, Jeffrey L., and Aaron Wildavsky. *Implementation*. Berkeley: University of California Press, 1973.

Price, Don K. *Government and Science*. New York: New York University Press, 1954.

———. *The Scientific Estate*. Cambridge: Harvard University Press, 1965.

Ransom, Harry Howe. *Can American Democracy Survive Cold War?* Garden City, N.Y.: Doubleday Anchor Books, 1964.

Reagan, Michael D. "The Political Structure of the Federal Reserve System," *American Political Science Review* LV (March 1961): 64–76.

Reedy, George E. *The Twilight of the Presidency*. New York: The World Publishing Co., 1970.

Rehfuss, John. *Public Administration as Political Process*. New York: Charles Scribner's Sons, 1973.

Riggs, Fred W. "Bureaucracy and Political Development: A Paradoxical View." In Joseph La Palombara, ed., *Bureaucracy and Political Development*. Princeton: Princeton University Press, 1963.

Ripley, Randall B. "Interagency Committees and Incrementalism: The Case of Aid to India," *Midwest Journal of Political Science* VIII (May 1964): 143–65.

Rogers, David. *110 Livingston Street*. New York: Random House, 1968.

Rourke, Francis E. *Secrecy and Publicity: Dilemmas of Democracy*. Baltimore: The Johns Hopkins Press, 1961.

———. "Bureaucratic Secrecy and Its Constituents," *The Bureaucrat* 1 (Summer 1972): 116–21.

———, and Glenn E. Brooks. *The Managerial Revolution in Higher Education*. Baltimore: The Johns Hopkins Press, 1966.

Rowat, Donald C. *The Ombudsman Plan: Essays on the Worldwide Spread of an Idea*. Toronto: McClelland and Stewart, 1973.

Saletan, Elma M. "Administrative Trustification," *Western Political Quarterly* XI (December 1958): 857–74.

Sayre, Wallace, ed. *The Federal Government Service*. Englewood Cliffs, N.J.: Prentice-Hall, 1965.

————, and Herbert Kaufman. *Governing New York City*. New York: Russell Sage Foundation, 1960.

Schaller, Lyle E. "Is the Citizen Advisory Committee a Threat to Representative Government?," *Public Administration Review* XXIV (September 1964): 175–79.

Schattschneider, E. E. *The Semisovereign People*. New York: Holt, Rinehart and Winston, 1960.

Scher, Seymour. "Congressional Committee Members as Independent Agency Overseers: A Case Study," *American Political Science Review* LIV (December 1960): 911–20.

————. "Regulatory Agency Control Through Appointment: The Case of the Eisenhower Administration and the NLRB," *Journal of Politics* 23 (November 1961): 667–88.

Schick, Allen. "The Road to PPB: The Stages of Budget Reform," *Public Administration Review* XXVI (December 1966): 243–58.

————. "A Death in the Bureaucracy: The Demise of Federal PPB," *Public Administration Review* 33 (March/April 1973): 146–56.

Schiff, Ashley L. *Fire and Water: Scientific Heresy in the Forest Service*. Cambridge: Harvard University Press, 1962.

Schilling, Warner R. "The H-Bomb Decision: How to Decide Without Actually Choosing," *Political Science Quarterly* LXXVI (March 1961): 24–46.

————. "Scientists, Foreign Policy, and Politics." In Robert Gilpin and Christopher Wright, eds., *Scientists and National Policy-Making*. New York: Columbia University Press, 1964.

Schubert, Glendon. *The Public Interest*. New York: Free Press of Glencoe, 1960.

Scott, Andrew M. "Environmental Change and Organizational Adaptation," *International Studies Quarterly* 14 (March 1970): 85–94.

Seidman, Harold. *Politics, Position, and Power*. New York: Oxford University Press, 1970.

Selznick, Philip. *TVA and the Grass Roots*. Berkeley: University of California Press, 1949.

————. *Leadership in Administration*. Evanston, Illinois: Row, Peterson & Co., 1957.

Shapiro, Martin. *The Supreme Court and Administrative Agencies*. New York: Free Press, 1968.

Sharkansky, Ira. "Four Agencies and an Appropriations Subcommittee: A Comparative Study of Budget Strategies," *Midwest Journal of Political Science* IX (August 1965): 254–81.

————. "An Appropriations Subcommittee and Its Client Agencies: A Comparative Study of Supervision and Control," *American Political Science Review* LIX (September 1965): 622–28.

Sigal, Leon V. *Reporters and Officials: The Organization and Politics of Newsmaking.* New York: D. C. Heath, 1973.

Simon, Herbert A. *Administrative Behavior.* New York: The Macmillan Co., 2nd ed., 1957.

———. *The New Science of Management Decision.* New York: Harper & Row, 1960.

———, Donald W. Smithburg, and Victor Thompson. *Public Administration.* New York: Alfred A. Knopf, 1950.

Sjoberg, Gideon, Richard A. Brymer, and Buford Farris. "Bureaucracy and the Lower Class," *Sociology and Social Research* 50 (April 1966): 325–37.

Skolnick, Jerome. *Justice Without Trial.* New York: John Wiley & Sons, 1966.

Smith, Bruce L. R. *The Rand Corporation: Case Study of a Nonprofit Advisory Corporation.* Cambridge: Harvard University Press, 1966.

Sorensen, Theodore C. *Decision-Making in the White House.* New York: Columbia University Press, 1963.

Steiner, Gilbert Y. *Social Insecurity: The Politics of Welfare.* Chicago: Rand McNally & Co., 1966.

Stillman, Richard J. "Woodrow Wilson and the Study of Administration: A New Look at an Old Essay," *American Political Science Review* LXVII (June 1973): 582–88.

Tanenhaus, Joseph. "Supreme Court Attitudes Toward Federal Administrative Agencies," *Journal of Politics* 22 (August 1960): 502–24.

Thayer, Frederick C. *An End to Hierarchy! An End to Competition!* New York: New Viewpoints, 1973.

Thomas, Norman C., and Harold L. Wolman. "The Presidency and Policy Formulation: The Task Force Device," *Public Administration Review* XXIX (September/October 1969): 459–71.

Thompson, James D., and William J. McEwen. "Organizational Goals and Environment: Goal-Setting As An Interaction Process," *American Sociological Review* 23 (February 1958): 23–31.

Thompson, Victor A. *The Regulatory Process in OPA Rationing.* New York: Columbia University Press, 1950.

———. *Modern Organization.* New York: Alfred A. Knopf, 1961.

Thomson, James C. "How Could Vietnam Happen? An Autopsy," *The Atlantic* 221 (April 1968): 47–53.

Truman, David B. *The Governmental Process.* New York: Alfred A. Knopf, 1951.

Waldo, Dwight. *The Administrative State.* New York: The Ronald Press, 1948.

Wamsley, Gary L., and Mayer N. Zald. *The Political Economy of Public Organizations.* Lexington, Mass.: Lexington Books, D. C. Heath and Co., 1973.

Wengert, Norman. *Natural Resources and the Political Struggle.* Garden City, N.Y.: Doubleday & Co., 1955.

Wildavsky, Aaron. *Dixon-Yates: A Study in Power Politics.* New Haven: Yale University Press, 1962.

————. *The Politics of the Budgetary Process.* Boston: Little, Brown and Co., 1974.

Wilensky, Harold L. *Organizational Intelligence.* New York: Basic Books, Inc., 1967.

Wilson, James Q. "Innovation in Organization: Notes Toward a Theory." In James D. Thompson, ed., *Approaches to Organizational Design.* Pittsburgh: University of Pittsburgh Press, 1966.

————. "The Bureaucracy Problem," *The Public Interest,* no. 6 (Winter 1967): 3–9.

————. *Varieties of Police Behavior.* Cambridge: Harvard University Press, 1968.

————. *Political Organizations.* New York: Basic Books, 1973.

Wynia, Bob L. "Federal Bureaucrats' Attitudes Toward a Democratic Ideology," *Public Administration Review* 34 (March/April 1974); 156–62.

Zeigler, Harmon. *Interest Groups in American Society.* Englewood Cliffs, N.J.: Prentice-Hall, 1972.

Index